Lords

Written by
William J. Ryan
P.O. Box 666
Dade City, FL.
33526
352-567-5900

--- **First Edition** ---

FADE IN:

CREDITS OVER:

EXT.   A STREAM IN A SMALL VILLAGE - MORNING

We see two small, frail looking children playing by a stream. The girl called Dora, has only one good eye and has trouble breathing. Yet she plays in the mud with her friend, unencumbered by her handicaps. As she builds a little mud house, she thinks of life when she will be all grown up, and has a husband and a home, like the one she had just made.

Her playmate, Joel, is throwing rocks into the water. He has trouble walking, because his foot is deformed. The rocks he throws do not go very far, because he doesn't have much strength. We can see that the water is not very clean. It is brown, more like a rust color. Even the rocks are stained by it. There are no fish, and no plants grow in the water any more.

At the top of an embankment is a small cemetery made with humble stones and handmade toys, marking the place where so many were born and died before the age of five. We see a young Latino woman named Marie sitting with her friend, stroking a white stone beside her. It is the marker for her most recent lost child.

We see the community farm, where stalks of corn are growing with a few scattered rows of tomato plants. In the background we can see several small homes that follow a dirt road. It's a small village that has around 100 people that live there.

CUT TO:

A large Latino man named Miguel, quietly walks up to the cemetery with his hat in his hand and pays his respects to all the dead. He sees the two women tending to the stones, pulling weeds and calls to his son Joel…

                    MIGUEL
          This is not a place to play. It is time
          to come and eat.

CUT TO:

We see Dora and Joel running as fast as they could run in their bare feet to catch up to Miguel. They are covered in dirt and mud, wearing undisciplined smiles that fill their faces. Right behind them is Marie and her friend.

PAN OUT:

The whole town has turned out for this day, all one hundred of them. Every eye in town is now on Dora and Joel, as they run up to Miguel.

They have become the center of the whole village. They are the only young children that remained. Muddy hugs and dirty-faced smiles are all welcomed. It's when Joel sees the whole village he remembers that his father Miguel, is leaving.

They all meet in the center of town, where tables have been set up under an old tree with lots of shade. The food was prepared for them, as well as something to drink, and extra food is packed away. The whole town has helped them, by sending them off with a good meal.

It is not a party, but a somber moment. Someone hands Miguel an old metal overnight case that is scratched up and tattered, it looks like it has seen many places. The village elder hands the case to him and a key on a chain, to be kept around Miguel's neck. No one says anything as they hug and shake hands. Miguel gives his boy a hug as though it were their last.

                              SOMEONE
                            (Yells)
              Let's eat!

They all dig in. They talk about the future putting all their hopes on Miguel. The burden is now his and he knows he must succeed for everyone, most of all, his son.

Miguel and another man named Peppy climb into an old truck. The floors are so rusty they can see the road under their feet. The right front fender is loose and rattles as they drive. The doors must be lifted up, in order to close and latch it. They sit on broken springs and seats that have been re-covered several times. Their packed bags rest between them, while Miguel holds the small case tight to his side.

The old truck starts in a puff of blue smoke as two of the women hand each man a cloth package filled with food for the long trip. The smell of good food fills the cab.

They take off and the truck disappears in a cloud of blue smoke and road dust. Only the sound of its motor and the rattles from the right front fender can be heard as they drive away. They have a long drive ahead of them and Miguel has put a lot of faith in this old truck.

CUT TO:

INT.   INSIDE THE PICK-UP - NIGHT - SEVEN DAYS LATER

For seven days and six nights, Miguel and Peppy have traveled. The entire time they were arguing.

                              PEPPY
              This is wrong and it's a foolish (more)

waste of time and money.

MIGUEL
(Smiles)
Everything will be fine.

PEPPY
(Argues)
You do not know how things will turn out
and you cannot say. We trusted before and
they cheated us. You know this to be true.

MIGUEL
Peppy, you need to trust people sometimes,
when things like this are beyond our
control.

Peppy feels strongly on this point.

PEPPY
Trust is no good. We have trusted people
in the past and look where we are!

They continue the argument as they have for the past few months.
After the 7th day of traveling and covered in a week's worth of road
dust from every road they have taken to get to this point.

MIGUEL
(Smiles)
This truck has been good to us. We've only
broken down twice so far, and we are almost
there.

Each day has been hot from the sun and cool at night. Some of the
roads were paved, but this last one is full of potholes and looked
seldom traveled.   Signs of other people are becoming nonexistent.

As the day ends, Miguel looks at the small hand-made map in his pocket.

MIGUEL
(Smiles)
That's the one, pull in there.

They pull into the small roadside motel. Years of dirt cover the
windows. Tree branches hang over the entrance, touching the ground.
It is old and rundown with siding boards falling off the side where
they've parked. They sit and look at how the wood is blistered from
the sun and how weeds have grown to five feet high in some places.

PEPPY
Are you sure this is right?

> **MIGUEL**
> Yes, it is the same address and the same
> name I was given.

They sit and look for signs of life. They see none as they shut off
the old truck, tired from its long journey. It seemed as though all
three sighed from the relief of getting to their destination. Peppy
strains to see through the dirt covered windows.

> **PEPPY**
> You wait here. I will go and see if this
> is the right place.

He gets out of the truck and slowly walks up to one of the windows
to peek in. A dark figure waves him in.

> **PEPPY**
> I will go in first, wait here.

Peppy walks up the weathered wooden steps, over to the front door
and as he's opening it, the door creaks and looks as though it had
not been used in years, but he continues on.

The dark man is brown from the sun, wearing a camouflage uniform with
a rifle over his shoulder. He puts a paper into Peppy's face, so
he can read it. There before him, are both Miguel's and Peppy's names
with a key for room number 238. The man just stares as Peppy slowly
picks up the key and then the man points the way as Miguel joins them.

CUT TO:

INT. ABANDONED HOTEL - NIGHT

Peppy looks down the hall to see where he was pointing and the man
turns and walks away. They both stand and stare at his back as he
slowly disappears out the back door and into the bush, leaving only
the sound of a few flies behind him.

Miguel and Peppy head down the hall to look for the room that the
key belongs to. Once there Peppy puts the key into the lock and opens
the door.

> **PEPPY**
> I will check out the room to make sure it's
> safe.

While Miguel waits he looks at his surroundings.

The floor of the hallway is worn out dark red linoleum, peeling up
in several places, revealing the planking that is exposed on each
side. The plaster has fallen at the end of the musty hall, and lies
in a pile on the floor. There is a hole in the ceiling that is

exposing the plaster lathing, stained with water. He enters the room and sees that it is not much better, because the ceiling looks much the same.

CUT TO:

INT. MOTEL ROOM – NIGHT

Following Peppy, we see that the walls are covered in a dark yellow, flowered print paper which is falling away in places revealing other layers of print under it. Water stains run down the outside wall, catching Peppy's eye as he tries to look out the yellow, almost rust colored window glass.

There are two beds made up in the room. Peppy pats one, making a cloud of dust. On the dresser, there are clean towels folded neatly and stacked by a dusty mirror. On the floor in the dust, Peppy spots fresh small human bare footprints that must have been left there at the same time as the clean towels.

>   **PEPPY**
>   (Whispers)
>   At least there is more than just the man
>   with the gun here, because I am sure that
>   this was made by a child or a woman, and
>   that's a good sign.

The silence is broken by the sound of dripping water. At first, Peppy thinks is coming from the roof, but then follows the sound into a small room with a tub and sink.

>   **PEPPY**
>   Well, we have water… a bath sure would be
>   nice.

As he turns the handle, rusty water comes pouring out and slowly turns to clean cool water.

>   **PEPPY**
>   Well if he were going to rob and kill us,
>   he could have by now.

Peppy walks back to the hall intending to wave Miguel into the room, but he ran straight into him instead. Miguel had followed him. Miguel and Peppy do not care about overall condition of things, because at this point they only want to take turns in the tub, to rinse the road dirt off of them and sleep in real beds. As the sun is setting, they speak softly, because they have not heard a sound other than themselves. No cars or trucks driving by, no people, just them and the sounds of nature outside.

As Miguel and Peppy stretch out on their beds, the room slowly fills with the smell of food. They both quietly leave the room and follow the smell. Once at the end of the hall, they peek around the corner of the doorway to the main room and find the source. There is a basket filled with a warm meal and drinks sitting on a table.

Like all the other floors in the building, the floor in the main room is covered in dust, so whoever left the basket left more of those small bare footprints. Peppy points them out and holds up two fingers, indicating two people. Miguel slowly walks up to the back door, hoping to catch a glimpse of the owners of the prints and to thank them.

MIGUEL
>(Yells)
>
>Thank you!

There is no reply, so Miguel and Peppy sit in the dust and eat.

MIGUEL
>(Smiles)
>See, I trust them. If they wanted to do
>us harm, they could have killed us before
>now. So relax and enjoy the meal. These
>are not bad people and they do not fear us
>either.

PEPPY
>(Angry look)
>If that is true then why do they not show
>themselves? Why hide from us like thieves
>in the dark?

With that said, two small lights click on, giving the place a silent, haunted and eerie look. Peppy looks around the room and says…

PEPPY
>What kind of place is this? There has been
>no one on that road since we got here. We
>are the only ones to come here, and it looks
>like we are the first in a long time.

MIGUEL
>(Smiling warmly)
>You forget the man with the gun and the two
>that brought us food tonight. Maybe they
>just don't want to be seen. Stop worrying
>and remember; we will sleep in real beds
>tonight.

With that the stretch out for some rest.

CUT TO:

INT. ABANDONED MOTEL – MORNING

As they are packing up the meager belongings, Peppy reiterates his
dislike of the plan.

> **PEPPY**
> (Angry)
> I still say we should not do this. You are
> nuts to trust this person! Who are these
> other people and why do they hide?

> **MIGUEL**
> (Shrugs his shoulders and smiles)
> The time is over for trusting. You know
> this to be true. How could we go back and
> face our people if we fail at this? Did
> you ever think of that?

Miguel see's that Peppy is still angry.

> **MIGUEL**
> We must do our best to make this work.
> There are many people involved in this.
> We are to do our job and trust in the others
> to do theirs.

Peppy finishes packing his only change of clothes, washed out in the
sink the night before. They sit and wait at the table while picking
over the food brought to them last night.

> **PEPPY**
> (Snaps)
> How long do we wait here for them? I don't
> like this… They are playing with us. We
> have been sitting here all day now. Not
> a word, not a sound. We were told it would
> be today, right?

> **MIGUEL**
> That is what I was told. Sit and wait and
> someone will come.

Suddenly a horn honks out front. Miguel smiles and turns to Peppy…

> **MIGUEL**
> See, there is much you don't know. If one
> will not show up, another will. Like you
> and me. If I can't make it, you must, and
> if you fail another will follow us.

> **PEPPY**
> (Grits his teeth with anger)
>If none of you will do this thing, I will
>kill him myself. With my bare hands, I
>will squeeze the life out of this man! You
>have my word on this!

Miguel tries to calm him down…

> **MIGUEL**
>You have a job and it's not to kill! Now
>get your things together. We have a
>ride.

The front door opens and a slender man smoking a cigarette stands there.

> **JOE**
>I am Joe, your driver. I am supposed to
>pick up two gents here. It looks like you
>two are them.

> **MIGUEL**
>Yes sir, we just need to grab our things.

> **JOE**
>Oh, you don't need to bring all your stuff.
>Ain't anyone left here in these parts but
>people like me and we ain't going to rob
>you.

With that said Miguel grabs the small metal case and smiles…

> **MIGUEL**
>Well then, let's go.

EXT. ABANDONED MOTEL - DAY

They followed Joe out and they see a 1963, sun-bleached turquoise Chevy Biscayne, 4-door wagon parked outside. As Joe gets in he yells out…

> **JOE**
>Hop in boys, its newer then the one you just
>drove up in.

They both jump in the back of the old car without saying a word. Taped to the dash was a picture of both of them. The road is full of twists and turns. Dead trees have fallen in the road and potholes at times were almost blocking the road completely. Miguel keeps looking at the road for any signs of others, but there are no homes, fires for cooking or even ruts in the road from other cars.

Miguel notes that just off the road now and then, are the remains of abandoned homes. Their frames are broken apart and overgrown with weeds, trees and vines. One house is twisted off its foundation and sits tilted to one side. No people. No signs of life anywhere.

After several slow miles, the two men look at each other. One sniffs the air and the other follows. There is something in the air. Joe sees them; he knows they don't know what it is. Joe sticks his head out his window and takes in a deep breath.

                         JOE
          Ah, I love the smell of the salt air.

With that, no more was said. The tree-lined back road opens up, and for the first time they see the Gulf of Mexico. The endless blue water fills their wide eyes, for they have never seen it before. They turn right and cross a long and old wooden bridge that is close to the water. Then the blue sky disappears and is replaced with more green trees. The air is heavy with the dampness, for it has just rained here. After another mile or so of travel, Joe turns down a dirt path.
                         JOE
          This is it.

CUT TO:

EXT. DIRT PATH - EVENING

Miguel and Peppy get out of the back of the old car, and Miguel thanks the man. Joe just smiles, reaches down to a bag sitting next to him and starts to pull something out. Peppy grabs his wrist to stop him. Joe just smiles and slowly removes a spray can of bug repellent, then looks at Miguel and hands him the can. He then reaches back in the bag and hands them a flashlight.

                         JOE
          I didn't think you would have brought either
          one of these, and you'll need both out here
          when the sun goes down.

Joe looks at Peppy, then back at Miguel.

                         JOE
          You had better stand in front of him. He
          could end up dead and ain't anyone going
          to care out here.

                       MIGUEL
               (Smiles)
          He is young and does not trust anyone.
          Please forgive him.

Joe looks at Peppy and says…

                    JOE
          You are lucky to have him with you. They
          did right to pick someone that is full of
          trust and one that is full of distrust. He
          will for sure, have your back, because he
          trusts no one else. Be safe and may God
          be with you.

Miguel and Peppy step away from the car as it backs down the road until they can no longer see or hear it. They head down the unused path. There is a ghostly silence to the land as they step over dead rotten tree branches and palm fronds. Their footsteps are the only sound being heard except for the occasional bird warning others of their presence. As they walk, each one becomes more aware of the sounds they are making, so they both try to be quieter. They never know who may be listening or watching.

Just a few feet away, they spot the remains of a black top road crossing their path. The remains are full of cracks and just under the leaves. They can still see the center paint strips showing the center of the road. As they look down each direction the road once traveled, all they see is over growth and brush. At this point they stand at the remains of their dirt road next to the remains of an old highway and wonder what happened.

They sit and rest in the cool shade and enjoy the sights and sounds of this strange and abandoned place. The air at most times, would grow still and heavy with silence.

                    MIGUEL
               (Points to his watch)
          We should stay until dark.

They didn't have long to wait. Soon they would need the bug spray.

                    MIGUEL
               (Checking his watch)
          It's time.

They head down the winding, twisty road, splashing in water that was trapped in holes in the pavement of a road, long ago abandoned. The trees would sometimes open up and let the moonlight in along the way. It helped illuminate the barely passable road.
Vines and dead limbs lay on the road as though they had been there for years, food for the termites. A large black snake was coiled up on a rock that's been baking in the sun all day.

Miguel's flashlight caught a glimpse of red eyes staring back at them from the water's edge and from thick trees over their heads. The air is thick with humidity and the maddening sound of mosquitoes.

The swarms, at times seem to fill the air, so they have to keep spraying bug repellant on themselves.

They continue traveling and come across a suspension bridge made of old wood and rusting cables. There are holes in the planks and it leans to the right. It doesn't look very sturdy. Miguel stops and looks it over. They decide to cross it slowly. Pieces of it fall into the returning tidewater gently flowing under it. Peppy does not like it, but continues. The bridge holds them and they keep heading down the barely observable road.

After some time, they can see a light off in the distance. They stand frozen for a moment, looking for signs of life, but there are none. It is a flickering light, so they know it's a fire. As they approach it slowly, they hear no sound. Yet, Miguel is sure they are being watched. They keep moving closer and still no signs of other people or sounds.

                    MIGUEL
                 (Whispers)
          What fire makes no sound?

Miguel could see that the fire flickering off the water, so it was a much smaller fire then he first thought.

Finally, they can see where the fire originates. It's a small pond, where a flame is coming out of the center of the water. It is the only light. The small white flame is almost blinding as they step out of the darkness into its light. The whole time Peppy has been whispering to Miguel.

                    PEPPY
          We are lost. You must have gone the wrong
          way. This is stupid.

They stood there looking at the flames for a few moments.

                    MIGUEL
                 (Points)
          See the water burning?

                    PEPPY
                 (Nods)
          Yes.
                    MIGUEL
          Now I know we are on the right road. Do
          you believe now? You said all this time,
          water will not burn. Do you see the water
          burning? It is as we were told. You must
          trust… you must believe.

Peppy said nothing, but was transfixed on the small blue and white flames that were about one to two feet high. They continue down a few hundred feet more and the path takes a sharp turn into a clearing. There is a large sand mound or dune. No trees, no grass, it is made up of old shells left by the Indians a thousand years ago.

As they slowly walk to the edge of the glade, they stand and look for signs of life, but there are none. Miguel continues to lead them slowly out of the woods and into the soft sand. At the top of the hill is the outline of a large black pyramid. The outline could be seen only because it was blocking the stars. The moonlight shining down upon them made the white sand bright as daylight.

As they walk up to the pyramid, they could see further down the beach, to the water's edge. There, at its edge, they see two large black towers next to the sea on each side of a large lagoon, where there is a boat dock and path leading to the pyramid. The beach seems to come right to the foot of the pyramid.

They walk on, taking a wide berth around the intimidating black pyramid, looking for any signs of life, foot prints… anything. But there are none. They walk down to the water, and stand there on the beach enjoying the soft breeze and notice that there are no mosquitoes buzzing in their ears. Miguel and Peppy still do not speak. They only look for someone to come out, but there is not a sound, just the water at the beach's edge lapping on the shore.

Miguel points to the pyramid and starts to walk slowly closer, still looking for an opening or any signs of life. Both are awestruck by the pyramid's shape, color and texture. Still there seems to be no doors or windows. Miguel stands in front of it at the end of the path from the black towers to the pyramid.

MIGUEL
(Whispers)
This must be where the door is.

Miguel, very slowly walks up to the corner and with one finger touches it. He is curious as to what it is made of. He breaks off pieces of rust, still warm from the sun, and knows it is made of steel.

MIGUEL
(Whispers)
Next to the ocean-this makes no sense.

Suddenly, from the center of the pyramid facing the side Miguel just touched, a large section opens in the middle, with a flat panel rising up from the base of the pyramid, creating an awning over an entryway. It reveals two, 10 ft high closed, brass doors next to smooth shiny black walls, with no rust.

Miguel and Peppy are frozen in place as they stand in front of the opening. It did not make a sound as it opened. Miguel turns to Peppy and softly speaks…

MIGUEL

Remember what I said, you say nothing.
Your temper will bring you no good.

They slowly walk over and stand under the cover, in front of the doors. They can see they are made of polished gold or bronze, and they can see themselves in its reflection. Again, without a sound, the doors slowly open inward revealing the silhouettes of two petite young women.

As their eyes adjust from the dim moonlight to the soft yellow light coming from inside, they can see that the two that answered the door, are barely dressed in what Miguel first thought must be, ancient Egyptian clothing. One begins to speak in the softest of voices…

TUP-CON

My name is Tup-Con and this is Lee-Yaa.

They both give them big friendly smiles.

PEPPY

(Whispers softly)
Those smiles are like those of a Jackal
before killing their prey.

Each young woman has jet black hair and black eyes, they could be twins. Their long hair pulled back and bound in ponytails. They both continue standing there with big smiles each holding one of the golden doors.

TUP-CON

Oh, we are so glad you are here; he has been
waiting for you.

The two girls walk up, each taking one of Miguel hands and one of Peppy's hands. They walk them in ever so gently, not making a sound. Miguel notices they both have the bodies of athletes. He can see the muscle tone reflecting off their skin in the dim light.

PEPPY V.O.

Her touch is so light; I can't even feel
her touching my hand. She is that gentle.

Miguel and Peppy notice how cool it is inside. They enter the hallway, looking at the black, polished, marble floors trimmed in gold. There were two large statues, both also made of marble. There were two lit torches on both sides of an entrance to another room. A flickering white firelight, coming from a large bowl on each side of this other room, fill it with a soft glow revealing murals on the walls, of a land they do not know. At the end of the room before them, is a large chair sitting on a carved platform it was a throne made of gold. There behind a gold mask, sits a muscular man wearing clothes of gold.

The flickering light enhances his eyes in the darkness. Tup-Con and Lee-Yaa lead them up to the middle of the room, facing the man in gold. They all stand there, saying nothing. Then the man in the partial mask shifts on his gold throne. His slender muscular body reveals the results of a good diet and hard work. Then in a very high pitched voice he speaks…

MAN IN MASK (LORD)
Miguel it is good to see you. Did you bring it?

MIGUEL
(Holding up the case)
Yes sir. I have it right here.

PEPPY
Are you for real? I keep telling everyone you're just a con and you're just going to steal our money! What kind of place is this? Who the hell are you?

The man in the chair does not move, his eyes widen, his veins rise on his neck, he leans forward and rises from his chair very slowly. He snaps his fingers. Tup-Con and Lee-Yaa run in from the shadows at both sides of his chair. Pointing his strong fingers at Peppy he says…

LORD
Take this one called Peppy, outside.

They run to Peppy without making a sound and gently taking both his hands, they start to escort him out. Lee-Yaa looks up at him and says…

LEEY-YAA
It is time for you to leave.

PEPPY
(Snarls)
I want to know; what are you really going to do?

Tup-Con and Lee-Yaa simultaneously, nearly snap off Peppy's small fingers and then push down on both of his elbows, dropping him to his knees in one quick move. Peppy lets out one ear piercing squeal as he is forced further down on the floor still on his knees. Tup-Con leans over and whispers in his ear…

TUP-CON
You are now going to walk out the door, on your knees. You see, it is time for (more)

you to go.

Miguel looks on silently in approval as Peppy is escorted from the room in great pain.

CUT TO:

EXT.   THE PYRAMID - NIGHT

Both Tup-Con and Lee-Yaa continually hold his small fingers on both hands. When he starts to struggle and fight back, there is one quick snap and both fingers are broken.

Peppy screams in pain, he is on the verge of passing out as he falls face down into the sand. He drifts in and out of consciousness with his face in the sand. Lee-Yaa lets go and runs and gets some tape, as Tup-Con holds on to Peppy's arm and turns him over. Lee-Yaa runs back. They both quickly reset the bones and start taping his broken fingers together to the next good finger on each hand. Peppy, who is now conscious sits in the sand, looks down at his hands, and notices again that he can barely feel their hands touching him.

> **TUP-CON**
> (Softly smiles)
> You are very lucky that he didn't ask to
> have you killed!

They helped him to his feet. Peppy returns their smiles and looks down at them, still taken in by their tender beauty.

> **PEPPY**
> You wouldn't do that… you couldn't.

Tup-Con and Lee-Yaa both open their belts at the same time and in a flash, Peppy finds two knives pointing at the juggler veins in his neck. With the blades pressing harder into his neck, he rises up on his toes and lifts his head to avoid being cut. Tup-Con's black eyes twinkle in the dark and she says…

> **TUP-CON**
> I would enjoy killing you. You have no idea
> just how lucky you are. We both have
> killed before and we would kill again… for
> our God! Besides, we have two black
> hungry pit bulls.

She points to the back of the hall where Peppy can only see two sets of red eyes.

> **LEE-YA**
> (Smiling)
> They are just sitting in the corner, (more)

restless, just waiting for a signal and you
will be dinner.

Tup-Con and Lee-Yaa pull back their knives, and he notices a small
drop of blood running down Lee-Yaa's blade. She licks it clean,
glaring back at him with her cold black eyes. She then looks hard
at Tup-Con, then back at Peppy. Then Tup-Con leans over to whisper
in Peppy's ear loud enough for Lee-Yaa to hear.

                    TUP-CON
                (Smiles)
          You see, you are lucky. Did you see what
          she did? She tasted your blood on her
          knife, I think she likes you.

While they finish attending to Peppy's wounds, and the three can hear
Miguel having a conversation back inside. Their voices echoing off
the walls are soft and in agreement. Peppy strains to hear what they
are saying as their voices echo off the walls, but he can't and says…

                    PEPPY
          I want to go back in.

                    TUP-CON
          That time is gone. You will wait in the
          back now.
                    PEPPY
                (Demands)
          No, I want to be with my friend.

Lee-Yaa pulls out her knife once more and starts lunging the blade
at his body in short jabs. Before Peppy can speak, he starts to take
one step back. He had already been shallowly stabbed five times in
the chest. He gives in saying…

                    PEPPY
          Ok, Ok, I will wait in the back.

CUT TO:

EXT. BEHIND THE PYRIMID - NIGHT

Once behind the pyramid, they tape his wounds without saying a word.
Then Tup-Con smiles at Peppy and says…

                    TUP-CON
          See, I was right. Lee-Yaa does like you.
          You're still alive; these are but small
          love cuts to remind you of your adventure
          this day.

Then simultaneously, they kick him behind the knees and he lands on his ass. Lee-Yaa points her knife at his throat saying…

                         LEE-YA
             Now, sit there or I will chop you up and
             feed you to the dogs.

Tup-Con stands on Peppy's left hand with her left foot, pressing down on his broken finger with her toes. Then she kneels down on her right knee to straighten Peppy's black hair out of his eyes.

                         TUP-CON
             Don't you ever speak to our Lord like that
             again, or I will kill you without warning.
             This is your only warning!

Peppy, grimacing in pain, with beads of sweat forming on his forehead, says not another word. This fight is over.

INT.   THE PYRIMID - NIGHT

Back inside, the Lord is still on his throne speaking softly in that high pitched tone…
                         LORD
             So it is understood. You will tell your
             people at the right time.

                         MIGUEL
             Yes, My Lord.
                         LORD
             Put the case on the table.

Miguel complies and sets it down.

                         LORD
             It will take you 7 days to get back. On
             that 7th day, have everyone ready. They'll
             be coming then. It will take them a week
             or two, but it will all be over then.
Just then, Tup-Con and Lee-Yaa appear back in the room standing next to Miguel.
                         LORD
             Tup-Con, tape the key to the top of the case
             and then tape the case shut. Give Miguel
             a marker. Miguel, sign your name over the
             top of the tape that seals the case.

She does as she is told and wraps both sides in tape. He too, does as he is told without question, but in his mind he wonders why. Sitting back onto his throne, Lord brings his thumb and index finger tips together and says…

                    LORD
          That concludes our business. Tell Peppy,
          it is because of my friendship with you
          that he is not dead. Make sure he
          understands. Also, I do understand his
          anger. We need him.

                    MIGUEL
               (Clenched his fist)
          I had higher hopes for this one. I wanted
          you to like him, but I thought he could
          control his anger. Please forgive him, I
          know you have already, but he just buried
          another child.

The Lord shakes his head and lowers his hands.

                    LORD
          That is also why he is not dead. I do
          understand, and tell him to get ready; I
          have a special treat in store for him.

                    MIGUEL
          I'll let him know, my lord.

The Lord spots the reflecting light off the eyes of the girls watching
and says…
                    LORD
          That is if the girls did not kill him. I
          don't hear any sounds, is he still alive?

Tup-Con and Lee-Yaa sprint up to the throne and quickly drop down
to their knees, bending down and their faces near the floor.

                    LEE-YA
          We did not kill him. He waits in the back
          guarded by the dogs. I feel he will show
          more respect next time, if he has this
          privilege again.

The Lord points to the sea.
                    LORD
          You both have had a hard few days. You can
          bed down in the tower. We have made
          arrangements for you both.

They all bow in respect and back out of the room without speaking.

CUT TO:

EXT. BEHIND THE PYRIMID - NIGHT

Peppy is still sitting outside wiping the blood from his neck, along with the five new wounds in his chest. Four of the small cuts have not quite closed yet. Miguel comes out and starts walking in the direction of the towers. Peppy gets up, without help and follows. They do not speak. As they near the first tower, they see the two dogs milling about, blocking the path. They look back at Tup-Con and Lee-Yaa. Tup-Con snaps her fingers one time and both the dog's hunch. The hair on their back raises and they begin to growl and snarl. Lee-Yaa claps her hands twice and they walk away. The girls both smile and go back into the pyramid. In the moonlight they can see the wall closing in silently. The door sealed closed, blocking all light from within.

MIGUEL

> The job is done.

The silhouette of a man standing at the end of the dock holding a rifle signals to them to come down. Miguel thinks it looks like the same man in the hotel. When they get to the end of the dock, they are standing next to one of the towers. It too is black, with no seams and completely covered in rust. The man with the gun opens the side and in the dim light coming from within they can see two cots. Miguel and Peppy enter and sit down.

CUT TO:

INT. TOWER - NIGHT

Miguel lets out a sigh.

MIGUEL

> That was a very stupid thing to do. I warned you to control your anger and not to speak. You embarrassed me and almost got yourself killed. I have a good mind to just leave you here. I thought after all we talked about, you knew better! From this point on, I have given him my word; you and I will never speak of this. Not this event, not this place, this never happened. I have given my word, if you tell anyone, I will kill you myself.

Peppy is taken aback by Miguel's anger. He said nothing, as he wonders how he knows such a man. They both settle in for some rest. The sea air blows through the small room and the sounds of the sea put Miguel fast to sleep. Peppy thinks of the day and all of his wounds. Then wonders why there are no mosquitoes here…

PEPPY   V.O.

> *There are no insects here at all; the wind*
> *from the water must be pushing them away.*

DISOLVE TO:

INT. THE TOWER - MORNING

Peppy opens his eyes and turns to see Miguel sitting on the cot next to him.

> **MIGUEL**
> You don't have much bruising on your fingers and they don't look broke, even though we both know they are.

Then Peppy smells food in the air…

> **PEPPY**
> Is that chicken I smell?

> **MIGUEL**
> Yes. Once more our host has seen to our needs. Get up. It's time to go. We must return.

On the floor, is a box like the one left in the motel… Peppy now knows who the small footprints belonged to. As they step out into the blinding sunlight, their eyes are drawn from the black, rusty towers to the pyramid. They walk towards it; there is not a sound to be heard, nor a person in sight. They continue to walk down the dock, past the pyramid and a small lean-to, and head back into the woods following the same path. The burning water is gone. The water is still, like the woods. There is no sign of life except for them. As the trail winds back, they notice more patches of blacktop with the remains of a white line.

As they climb over the familiar dead tree lying across the road, they know they are getting close to the main dirt road where they had last had seen the driver, Joe. For the first time since the tower they speak…

> **PEPPY**
> We couldn't be so lucky as to have Joe with the old car show up again could we?

> **MIGUEL**
> Yeah, it's still a long walk if we can't get a ride.

As they make the last turn they both spot the back of that same old car, parked where he had dropped them off.

> **JOE**
> Hop in boys, unless you want to walk.

They both quicken their pace and get in the back of the car.

                    JOE
          (Sniff's the air)
     That food sure smells good. They do treat
     people right don't they?

                    MIGUEL
          (Smiles)
     Yes, they are very good hosts. Would you
     like some?
                    JOE
     No thanks, I have eaten.

Peppy just looks at his taped up hands and he rubs his finger over
one cut as he thinks, 'treat people right?'

                    MIGUEL
     So tell us, what is this place? We noticed
     the remains of an old black top road back
     there.
                    JOE
     Oh that's what's left of the highway.
     This was quite a nice place back in its day,
     they tell me. Your hotel is close to 100
     years old. It survived the hurricane of
     34, when much around did not. Then this
     place tried to come back. The old man that
     owned it was killed in the next big
     hurricane of 56.

He points to the remains of wood homes and some brick chimneys that
are over grown with the forest.

                    JOE
          (Continues)
     Yeah there were over 800 dead and no help
     came. That's when the place died and
     Mother Nature took it all back. It's all
     government land now.

As the driver pulls back up to the old hotel, the Victorian building
takes on a look of sadness.
                    JOE
     We still find human bones left by that
     storm. I try to give them some type of
     burial, so they're not just lying on top
     of the earth.

Miguel and Peppy don't know how to respond, finally Miguel speaks…

                    MIGUEL
     That is sad to hear, are there many (more)

like yourself that came back?

Joe looks out the window…

> **JOE**
> At first a few, but now it's only me here locally. I have the whole place to myself… mostly. I am a squatter and caretaker of sorts. They know I am here and they leave me alone.

Peppy gets out of the car and Miguel joins him, both thanking Joe as Peppy walks away.

> **MIGUEL**
> Thank you for the lift. How much do we owe you?

> **JOE**
> It's all covered. Good luck on your long drive back. Be safe.

He drives off and they return to their room. There on Peppy's bed is a first aid kit.

> **MIGUEL**
> So it is true. Seems the girls like you after all.

The room is just as they left it. Their bags are right where they left them by the door. Peppy sits down and cleans up his cuts that are still draining.

DISOLVE TO:

EXT.   THE VILLAGE – DAY

Seven days later they arrive back at the small village.

> **MIGUEL**
> Everybody needs to get ready; they are coming soon.

> **PEPPY**
> I believe that they only wanted the money. They are never going to come. I tried to ask questions and they almost killed me. Look what they did to me! They are never going to show! You are all fools to believe in them and trust them! They only want the money!

Miguel sits down in his home surrounded by family and friends as he tells of his exploits. Before Peppy could climb into bed and get some badly needed sleep, dozens of trucks showed up pulling heavy equipment. The construction men were sickened by the sight of the pollution and angered over the cemetery for babies. All the men, like the villagers, doted over Dora and her friend Joel.

The first job was to repair and widen the road. Then west of the small town they leveled the earth and brought in fresh black dirt for farming. Diverting the pollution away from the stream was top priority as a holding pond was created on the polluters land.

By now there must have been over 100 men working to make their community better. But the biggest project was to cut a new path for the stream. Much of the rusty dirt was removed and piled on the source of the pollution. The toxins were then covered with more rock and dirt until it could be seen no more. The air turned clean and life returned to the land. It took the crew next to no time to repair the land and make things conductive for people to live.

A place where the land was clean and now protected from the toxins, the spring water flowed. Then workers worked by a glade of large trees to make a park. The trees grew next to large rocks on a hillside that no one wanted. It was no good for planting food, so it was easy to turn it into a park. The men made a swing set for the kids.

All the men of the town pitched in and tried to help. The women would bring water and food, in spite of the crews portable cook house. At the end of each day, they all would get together to eat and speak of the progress.

They made the stream wider near the small town. Its banks tapered, now smoothly down to the clean, flowing, water with fresh unsoiled earth. It would flow down to a dam that would hold water for dry times. The water would help to build a small lake.

The foundations were being laid for new buildings. Plans were to make a community center for all the villagers. But most important was the small hospital and school.

They kept going until the lowlands next to the village, were raised several feet. The new topsoil will grow much better corn and add a couple of feet to its height for producing a better harvest. The smell of fresh new dirt filled the air. Then it happened. Coming down the newly dug path, they see beautiful, crystal, clean, water. The smell of death and the toxic, brown, water, was no more.

DISOLVE TO:

EXT. VILLAGE CENTER – DAY

Three days later, Miguel looked at Peppy as the water pooled in the new reservoir and said…

MIGUEL
Do you still think he is just going to steal
from us?

PEPPY
(Looks down)
But how can he do all this on the small
amount we gave him?

MIGUEL
Next time you see him, you can ask him.
But I suggest you say nothing.

END SCENE

INT. BATTERY FACTORY - DAY

A few weeks later, in Los Angeles, California, a man prepares to sell his battery business. He waits anxiously at his desk. This is a big moment for him and he wants the money desperately. He walks to the window every few minutes, looking for his new buyer to arrive. He has never met him, so he wants to get a good look at him first. What matters to him most is the money.

> **MAN**
> (Whispers)
> I want to get away from this place and its smell. As far as that money will take me.

A black car pulls up to the gate of the plant, but he can't see anyone inside, because the glass is black. He puts on his suit jacket and sits behind his desk. He wants to be in charge. He is planning his departure from the building for the last time, while running over in his mind his departing check list.

Six people get out of the car, all dressed in black suits and ties. They start looking around. One slender man's figure stands out, as he gives orders. It's the arrival of the Lord, but he has taken on a new form in order to buy the factory. Standing at his side are Tup-Con and Lee-Yaa, holding onto his every word.

They are greeted and shown to the owner's office upstairs. As our Lord, now a man named Jule walks into the room showing his powerful personality. He starts talking about the purchase, the money, the transfer, the account numbers, and then Jule gives the seller a hard cold look and says...

> **JULE (LORD)**
> But I only have one concern...

Now, leaning on the owner's desk saying...

> **JULE**
> You opened up a plant in Mexico for recycling your wasted battery acid.

> **JOHN (OWNER)**
> Well that was a very profitable move for me. This is a battery recycling plant you know, and growth is part of all business. We are one of the largest in California. This waste water treatment that the Gold Coast Water Management orders, is extremely expensive. I can't tell you how much money I have saved doing it this way; by storing it in Mexico until we can get the proper recycling facilities to (more)

process the waste.

Jule stands erect again and slightly tilts his head to one side saying…

> **JULE**
> Near as I can estimate, you have been shipping 55 gallon drums down there for over 10 years. What seems to be the delay?

John smiles and looks out the window saying…

> **JOHN**
> Well, I'm not really going to ever treat that problem. I just got rid of the problem. Pollution removal costs a lot of money in America. By taking it down there, I save a lot of money and soon you will see what I mean.

He turns his eyes back to meet Jules…

> **JOHN**
> Besides it's not hurting anyone. I actually help that country by creating jobs; after all, I built a building didn't I?

Miguel steps up from the back and says…

> **MIGUEL**
> That's not what my records show! My researchers found that those drums are rusting away and pouring the acid onto the ground. It then travels down into a stream that feeds a small village and many more villages beyond that one. Your pollution is causing birth defects and stillborn children. I am also aware of a report that was given to you 5 years ago that clearly outlines the effects you are causing. Yet, you aren't willing to do anything to fix it. It's only money you save, but at what cost to others?

> **JOHN**
> (Looking up at Miguel)
> You don't understand business very well do you? The pollution would just naturally take care of itself; it would evaporate harmlessly into the air, being absorbed in the atmosphere. Have you seen that (more)

place? Who would want to live there? The dirt is so poor that you could not grow anything. It is a waste of land and that is why I picked that spot. It will just dry on the rock and will simply go away. The EPA makes such a big deal about it; there is nowhere else in the world that worries about this type of problem. The goal is economic growth. People need to understand that. If you are squeamish, then I will look into it and promise that I will try and do something. Or better yet, we can just take the land out of the deal. I don't care.

> **JULE**
> (Laughs)
> You really don't have to concern yourself with it anymore, because I have already taken care of it.

> **JOHN**
> (Pushing papers toward Jule)
> Good then let's move on. I have everything ready for you to sign…

John slowly lifts his head and looks directly at Jule. At that moment, another man walks into the room, but is unnoticed by John. Things are not going as he hoped and he is becoming concerned. John thinks of what Jule said…

> **JOHN**
> Just what do you mean when you say you've "taken care of it?"

Jule turns to ensure the door is closed. He then turns to look at the man that just came in. It is Peppy and he is carrying a small black case. Jule smiles at him, then turns to Tup-Con and Lee-Yaa and nods his head. They each smile at John and then walk to the front of his desk, each grabbing one John's arms and pulled him forward on the desk then they hold him there tightly.

> **JOHN**
> (Raises his voice)
> What do you people think you are doing? I am not about to be manhandled by you people! We have a contract stating you are buying the business including the buildings. I don't want to hear about problems. They are your problems now. It's just the way corporations work. It's the bottom line. How much money do (more)

you make? That's what it is all about?

The two girls still have John's arms, so they stretch him out over the desk, knocking everything on the desk to the floor. With his arms held tight over the top of the desk, he couldn't move. Miguel stood behind him, holding him in the chair and leaning on his head, pressing his face down to the desktop. He stops for a moment, watches Peppy who is now looking hard at John.

Jule flashes a rare big smile on his face, as Peppy walks slowly over to the desk and hands Jule the case. John is screaming and squirming as Jule slowly pulls out a nail gun, with 8 penny nails loaded in it. He slowly turns, puts the gun in Peppy's hand and smiles.

                         JULE
          This moment is for you. It is my gift to
          you.

Peppy smiled back and for the first time understood what power Jule has over Miguel. He slowly pressed the nail gun against John's wrist, with the pulling of the trigger drives one 8 penny nail through John's hand. It shatters the glass top. Then he does another one by his elbow. Then he repeats the same process on the other hand. John is nailed to the desk. He repeats his action counting out, until he reaches 30. Peppy's anger seems to be gone when he said…

                         PEPPY
          We have buried 30 babies.   Dead, as a
          result of your business, many more of our
          people have got cancer and breathing
          ailments. All so you can have more money
          and a better life! You are a murderer!

Jule steps forward as Peppy steps back…

                         JULE
             Just so you know, I have no intentions
          of buying your business, but I did need all
          of your account numbers.   The only way I
          was able to get them, was to pretend to be
          a buyer and agree to almost anything you
          wanted.
             Not only am I not buying your
          business, but I have already stripped it
          of every asset I could get my hands on.   I
          have already emptied all your accounts.
             Each one of your employees is under
          the impression that I am the new owner.   I
          have given them all a nice severance
          package. Everything that is in your name
          is now in my name and already sold (more)

> to someone else.
>
>   The lead on the shelves for the
> batteries is already sold. As we speak,
> trucks have loaded and are leaving with the
> new owners. I have remortgaged your home
> and this building all in your name. What
> you don't understand John, is that
> identity theft is so easy when you are
> dealing with greedy people like you. It is
> not hard at all!

As they start to walk out, Jule points out to Peppy several nice new car batteries sitting on the floor out in the hall.

JULE

Place one of those on the desk and pop open the cells, then dump it over and let the acid pour out towards John's face. Let him breathe what you have smelled all these years.

Peppy smiles and sets all four on the desk saying…

PEPPY

Here is another present for you.

Peppy then reaches down and picks up another car battery, pops the tabs and tips it over under his face.

PEPPY

Here, this is what we have been breathing; now you breathe it!

Then he dumped the rest on his head.

The acid that is pouring in John's lap is burning his flesh. He is screaming and squirming. They all quietly walk out the door. The plant is emptying; they are the last people to leave. Before they climb into the limousine, Jule dials 911 and informs them that he hears screams coming from the warehouse. Then he tosses the phone into a burning drum by the guard shack and they drive away.

DISOLVE TO:

EXT. THE VILLAGE - EVENING

We see a clean babbling brook with no rust stains or foul odor. There is new black soil with irrigation and plants popping up everywhere. A new community center just being finished. Still in progress is a school and small hospital, almost done. The construction crew is gone. They leave the villagers to finish the trimming of the construction.

That night, Peppy's shadow touches the walls of the community center in the full moon's light. No more the stench of battery acid and filthy drinking water. Life is good again. The full moon reminds him of the night they don't talk about. He rubs his chest feeling the scars left by Lee-Yaa's quick hand and knife.

He goes to bed and falls straight to sleep and dreams of that night. Deep in his sleep, he dreams that Tup-Con and Lee-Yaa slip ever so quietly into his bedroom through his window, and now stand next to the bed where he sleeps. They pull out their two daggers, holding them in both hands, together they jab them into his stomach. He screams, jumping up in bed and opens his eyes while holding his chest. The room is empty except for him and his wife, who is startled awake.

PEPPY'S WIFE

What's wrong Peppy?

He wipes the sweat from his brow as he looks around the room and out the window.

PEPPY

Oh, it's just a bad dream, it's nothing.
You go back to sleep.

He lays there and tries to fall back to sleep but he can't. He gets up and walks outside into the moonlight. The moon is still lighting the ground around him. He smiles as he walks into the community center rubbing his belly and then notices something that wasn't there before.

At the end of the room is a lone desk and on it sits a crate. He walks up to the crate made of a hard wood. There are no marks on the box and no labels. He tries to lift it, it wasn't very heavy and wasn't very large. He sits down and stares at the small crate, remembering the dream he just had.

He waits by the box. People start to stir as the sun comes up and his wife starts looking for him. With help, they find him in the community center, just sitting there. Slowly they start entering the room, and then someone asks…

MAN'S Voice

What is it?

PEPPY

I don't know. I couldn't sleep so at about
4:00 a.m. I came in here and there was this
box. Does anybody know whose it is or what
it is?

Everyone shakes their head side to side indicating no. They decide
to open it. They pry it open and there, inside, is the old scratched
up suitcase with tape all around it and a key with a signature still
in place, never opened. There was a small note under the case, Miguel
reads it.

NOTE READS
We are returning this to the people it
belongs to.

Miguel and Peppy just look wide eyed at each other. The case
contained their $10,000.00. It was every cent he and his neighbors
could get together to pay the Lord to help them.

Peppy rubbed his chest as he stood there looking at the case, then
slowly backed up so the others could see the box, because there was
something he had to do.

He slipped away unnoticed and went back to his home. There alone
he raised his shirt to check to see if his dream was real or just
in his mind.

There in the dim morning light he could see two new red marks on his
belly, just where he dreamt Tup-Con and Lee-Yaa had just stabbed him.
He then quickly turned to his bedside and look at the floor and there
in the dust by the window were those same foot prints he saw at the
hotel.

PEPPY
No, it can't be. These were made by
someone here.

To check he leaned outside his window and there in the dry powdery
dirt were two sets of bare foot prints.

PEPPY
It *was* them.

Peppy can hear his neighbors' joy over all the good fortune that has
come their way. As he stands there looking out the window at the
new foot prints running away and disappearing among the others he
thinks…

PEPPY   V.O.
This man didn't need their money after all;
He pulled millions out of the battery plant
and John. Who now, if still alive, must
have a breathing problem and acid burns
over half of his body.

Lifting his shirt, he runs his fingertips over the newest marks on
his belly. Two fresh slits barely breaking the skin were reminders
of his dream. Looking to the floor still there in the dust were those
barefoot prints. As he raised his head to look out the window, his

eyes following the trail, he said aloud…
PEPPY
> Whatever he asks, whenever he asks it, I
> will do whatever he wishes. You have my
> word.

The sounds of joy coming from the people were filling the streets, bouncing off the walls and coming into his room. Sounds not heard in a long time, bringing a smile to Peppy face.

END SCENE

INT.   PYRAMID - MORNING

Only the Lord's eyes were open in the dim light while Lee-Yaa and Tup-Con slept. His mind was on events yet to come. A photo hung across the room to remind him of who he is and what must be done every day. As he stared at it he thought…

LORD   V.O.

> *The time grows near and there is much yet*
> *to be done.*

Lord looked to his right and there was Tup-Con sound asleep, and to his left was Lee-Yaa, twitching as she does when she is dreaming. At his feet were the two pit bulls, both looking up at their master, here he ruled all. He knew he must lead if people were to follow.

Tup-Con and Lee-Yaa deserved to rest, they both did a good job. He slipped out of bed and entered the workroom downstairs. As he sat in the control chair he checked all the gauges and both towers were working as they should. His mind turned to the events yet to unfold. There was correspondence that he had not opened from the time they were gone.

As he flipped through the small stack, he found the one from Spain that he had been waiting for. At the moment Cusi (meaning joy) and Urpi (meaning dove) came in and wanted to be scratched and rubbed. He took time to give them their rewards and to let them outside.

He pressed a button on his remote and opened the back wall, much like the front, it opened to the outdoors. The heat of the day poured in, along with the bright sunlight. Cusi and Urpi ran and played as he read. When finished he talked aloud…

LORD

> This is good news and that means almost all
> of the pieces are in place. We are getting
> close and this is one more part to fit into
> the timeline.

On his map of the world, he placed a red circle around a city in Spain. It was then that he smiled; as he tapped the map he says out loud…

LORD

> Soon it will be your turn.

He then stood there motionless with his eyes glazed over, deep in thought. Then he backed up and his eyes ran over each small mark on the map that only he knew the meaning of. As his eyes moved from mark to mark, he was checking and rechecking each event that was to unfold in its timeline.

His concentration was broken by the awareness of a presence behind him. Without turning around, he said…

> **LORD**
> You did a very good job Tup-Con, you both
> did.

Behind him stood both girls, Lee-Yaa coming up behind Tup-Con standing in the doorway. They were used to his seeing behind him and knowing things no one else would know, for he was a god and gods see all.

Each morning was the same and the girls made food to feed the hungry that support all of them. They could see one of the two guards that spend all night watching them, moving behind a tree off in the woods. The Lord says…

> **LORD**
> It is time to feed the body. Some may have
> missed your cooking.

They both looked down and backed away to begin their task as he slipped back into the darkness to sit alone on his throne and think. As his mind raced over each event that was coming up, he lost track of time.

Tup-Con approached and silently stood before him holding something in both her hands. He looked up…

> **LORD**
> What is it?

> **TUP-CON**
> The guards need to talk to you.

She turned up the speaker on the walkie-talkie that she was holding. She then pressed the talk button…

> **TUP-CON**
> (Talking into the microphone)
> Go ahead.

> **GUARD**
> Yes, there is a small boat coming your way
> with two on board.

Lord sat up straight.

> **LORD**
> Good, prepare to greet them.

Tup-Con backed out and hurried to get all in place.

CUT TO:

EXT.   ON THE WATER – DAY

A small cabin cruiser could be heard coming around the mangrove trees, as it turned and pulled up to the dock.   A large man was at the helm and a tall slender blonde is with him.   He smiled at her and said…

                    LARGE MAN
          Let's go exploring.

She just smiled back, then awkwardly jumped out and tied off the boat as he instructed.   Both of them are now on the dock. They stand there looking around for signs of life.

CUT TO:

INT.   PYRAMID – DAY

Inside, Lee-Yaa watched them on the monitors from the work room and announced their movements.
                    LEE-YA
          They're trying to open the south tower and
          now walking up the dock, heading for us.

The back is sealed as they walk around the outside examining their find.   Cusi and Urpi, at both sides of their master, gave a small growl, because they knew someone was out there.   The couple was back at the front, about to give up, they turned to walk away.

                    LEE-YA
          They're heading back to the boat.   She is
          looking back.
                    LORD
          Good, open the door.

                    LEE-YA
          Yes, my Lord.

And with that said, she pressed a button and the front opened as silently as before.   The woman was awe struck as she watched it open without a sound.   She got the attention of the man that was with her, he too was now looking.
                    LEE-YA
          They are coming back.

Everyone was in place as the visitor's shadows filled the doorway and slowly crept across the entry floor, where the Lord could see them.   Tup-Con on his right and Lee-Yaa on is left, both lit the water torches filling the room with an eerie light.

                MAN FROM BOAT
          Is anyone here?

The girls stood with their backs to the wall by the doorway to the throne room.

> **BLONDE WOMAN**
> Wow! Burt, the floor is cool, there must be someone here. Hello, anyone home?

They kept walking in slowly, until they both stood in view of the Lord. No one moved.

> **BLONDE WOMAN**
> What is this place?

Hearing no response, she said…

> **BLONDE WOMAN**
> I don't like it, let's go.

> **BURT**
> No, we have come this far.

Burt took her hand and pulled her behind him. As they approached, Cusi and Urpi stood motionless and let out small growls. They froze in place and watched the man, wearing all gold and a gold mask turn in his chair. The blonde's hand now pulled on Burt's, as she tried to back away…

> **BLONDE WOMAN**
> We were just cruising by and spotted the place and were just curious as to what it was or is. We meant no harm. We will be leaving now.

The man's eyes, darted around, looking for something and then he too started to back up, knowing the damage those dogs could do. As they both turned they spotted the two girls glaring at them. The anger on their faces stopped the visitors in their tracks. The woman raised her hand in a defensive manner…

> **BLONDE WOMAN**
> We are sorry, we meant no harm. We will leave.

As they slowly walked back out into the sunlight, they tried adjusting to the light. The girls were right behind them and with one snap of the Lord's fingers; the girls raise their dart guns and hit both visitors in the neck.

> **BLONDE WOMAN**
> Burt, what the…

Moments later all went black.

END SCENE

INT.   THE PIT - DAY

The battered blonde woman rubbed her hand over old scars and sores, and rubbed her aching shoulder. As she sat up, pulling the twigs and leaves from her hair, she felt a small lump on her head. Then she noticed that she was naked, lying in the dirt with her ankles chained together.

A buzzing sound filled her head as she tried to open and focus her eyes. But she still couldn't see, because there was dirt in her eyes. As she tried to remove the dirt, she felt pain in her shoulder. Her heart started pounding as she saw that her leg was cut and covered with dried blood. Now she remembered, as she rubbed the sore spot on her neck from the dart, still in place.

She spotted Burt and started to crawl through the fog in her head toward him and her eyes darted around at the walls as she tried to wake him. Images from her childhood started racing back into her head and a look of horror came over her face as she stared at the walls.

BLONDE WOMAN

(Whispers)
This is a basement.

There was different colored paint where walls once stood, dividing off the rooms. The walls had been removed, because they would have provided a means to get out. The floor was covered in leaves, broken glass, rotting lumber and trash. It was uneven and tilted down to one side where standing water was home for a snake. She cradled Burt's head in her lap rocking him, as tears streamed down her face. She said to herself…

BLONDE WOMAN

Where has this guy taken me? What have I
stepped into now.

Burt too was naked, his overweight body was also covered in scratches and his feet were chained like hers.

BLONDE WOMAN

You're a nurse, do your job.

She snapped at herself, fighting off the drug and checking his vitals. He too was alive but out cold. She thought of what drug must have been in the dart as she rubbed her neck and then noticed her left arm.

BLONDE WOMAN

They drew blood from me.

She checked Burt and he had the same mark, where blood had also been drawn. Just then a shadow moved on the floor of the pit, her eyes darted up and she saw a man covered in camouflage with a rifle just standing there watching.

> **BLONDE WOMAN**
> What do you want? We don't have much
> money, but you can have it all.

He said nothing.

> **BLONDE WOMAN**
> They have all our money. That was dumb of
> me. What do they want from us?

She then reached down to see if she may have been raped, but it did not feel like it. Burt stirred and moaned in pain.

> **BLONDE WOMAN**
> Good you're alive! Don't leave me alone
> in here.

The shadow moved away as Burt stirred more and tried to sit up.

> **BLONDE WOMAN**
> No, don't move too much. Whatever the
> drug was, it will take time to wear off.

She looked closer and saw he has two marks on his neck.

> **BLONDE WOMAN**
> They must have hit you twice because you're
> bigger.

As he lay there, trying to fight off the effects he asked…

> **BURT**
> Where are we?

> **BLONDE WOMAN**
> I don't know… some kind of pit…

> **BURT**
> (Demanding)
> Describe it to me!

> **BLONDE WOMAN**
> The walls are stone, like a basement, but
> higher. There are dead leaves and
> branches all around us covering the floor.
> There is old trash and broken furniture.
> The walls were painted green, over white,
> over gray. And there is some kind of mold
> on them.

> **BURT**
> That is just like a woman; do the (more)

colors match the furniture?

BLONDE WOMAN
I am sorry, what do you want from me?

BURT
I can't see. So is there a way out that
you notice?

BLONDE
The walls look to be ten feet high.
Someone has added block to the walls to
make them higher, part of the floor is sunk
in and it's full of water.

He tried to look but the sun was too bright and it was all a gray
blur.

BURT
Can you help me sit up?

As she helped lift his head and he slowly straightened up, he said…

BURT
Oh man the whole place is spinning.

BLONDE
Just hold on and fight the drug, it will
pass.

As she looked around, she said…

BLONDE
There is a wall behind us we can lean on
and get out of the sun.

They scooted back into the shade and he began to regain control. As
they sat there listening to the sound coming over the walls, they
tried to hear any human voices they could call out to.

BURT
(Rubbing his eyes)
What do you remember Janet?

BLONDE/JANET
Not much. There was…

BURT
Shhhhh!

Off in the distance they could hear flutes playing. The sound was
growing closer. There was the sound of movement in the dried foliage
above as the sound of the flutes grew closer and closer.

The first one they could see, in front of the outside wall was Tup-Con, marching to the rhythm of her flute playing. Then, the man in gold came, followed by Lee-Yaa playing the same song.

They stood there looking down at their new guests, as the guard reappeared. His shadow was cast on the floor, only this time joined by another. Cusi and Urpi were playing, but jumped up and looked over the wall at their guests. Then, the Lord loudly clapped his hands twice and the flute playing stopped. He stood there over them without saying a word. Then Burt yelled up…

> **BURT**
> (Yelled)
> I am a police officer, they will be looking
> for me!

He got no response.

> **BURT**
> I don't know what kind of religious nut
> jobs you people are here, but one of you
> needs to do the right thing and call the
> police for help. I promise the one that
> helps us will not go to jail.

No one spoke. Then for the first time the blonde was aware there were mosquitoes in the pit and the silence was broken with a swat. Once more he clapped twice and points at the two men standing off to the side. It was then, one of the shadows moved back and she could hear his footsteps coming near them as he stopped just over their heads. She strains to try to see and she moved closer to Burt for safety.

Several days' worth of garbage was dumped on them from above. Some type of slimy, thick, brown water mixed with bones and other uneaten food, covered them. Flies now added to the mix of insects joining them in their pit. Still no reaction from above.

> **BURT**
> What the hell kind of people are you? You
> can't do this to people.

The guard returned to his place next to the other man and they all just stood looking down. Janet then joined Burt.

> **JANET**
> You don't have the right to do this to
> people. We are hurt and need medical
> treatment. We are people just like you!
> My mother is old and needs my care. I must
> get back to her.

She was thinking of her training for rape victims, trying to show
them...

                         JANET
          (Pleading and wiping muck from her eyes)
               We are human too. Please let us go. We
               won't tell anyone. We have family too.
               You shouldn't do this to people. It is
               wrong!

The Lord pointed to Tup-Con, then at the people in the pit. She
stepped forward...

                         TUP-CON
               We are not doing this to people. We are
               doing this to the Christians.

Suddenly they both looked at Burt's golden cross around his neck...

                         TUP-CON
               Yes, we'll let you keep the symbol of your
               god. Now you need to eat up. It may be
               your last meal and you will need your
               strength for what is to come.

With that said she stepped back and he clapped two more times. They
turned and, to the sound of flutes, paraded away, leaving only the
sound of insects and the smell of rotting food.

As night began to fall, Burt pointed out the small red lights on four
cameras pointed at them. They used the stagnant water to wash off
the slime from the trash. She found an old table cloth to help cover
them from what was to come. They cleaned out a corner and huddled
together for safety.

For her, the darkness oozed out of every crack until the black owned
the night. The light from the stars helped to keep back the memories
of her past.
                         JANET
                    (Whispering)
               See, it is not the same. We can see the
               stars. It's not the same.

As darkness wrapped around her the past filled the room and she
slipped back into her old survival mode.

                         JANET
                    (Whispered)
               I have survived before, I can do this
               again. I know how, now.

CUT TO:

INT. THE PIT — MORNING

The sun rose and the darkness slipped back underground. Janet awoke to find their bodies covered with insect bites. As she quickly checked for any that might be dangerous, she looked around for new dangers.

Burt, who was still asleep, had an equal amount of bites that seemed harmless so far. But he was warm and seemed to be running a fever. She stood up and started to walk around stretching her sore limbs and checking for signs of life other than the ones they had met so far.

She picked the last chicken bone out of her sticky, once blonde hair, and looked for a way out, but could find none. As she dragged her chains across the floor they got hooked on an anchor bolt once used to hold up a wall. She was painfully reminded of them and stopped to study them closely. They were shackles made for human beings, shaped so they will not cut into the flesh of the ankle but riveted together. No key would unlock them. They were not meant to be removed easily. Burt started to wake up.

> **BURT**
> Oh man, my head is killing me.

> **JANET**
> (Snapped)
> That's good to know. By the way, I am doing fine, thanks for asking.

He rubbed his head and tried to sit up…

> **BURT**
> Sorry.

> **JANET**
> Oh and you're not the first man that was only concerned about himself in my life. But you are the first to get me in a spot like this.

Her anger was replacing her fear, Burt thought. As he looked over the shackles and how they are secured, he said…

> **BURT**
> (Softly)
> No, I meant sorry for getting you into this spot.

> **JANET**
> Well this was your so-called quick, fun boat ride of a day on the water. I'll get you back before night. You knew (more)

just what you were doing.

As she watched him continue to determine how well they are locked
in place, she commented…

> **JANET**
> They are riveted and unless you have a
> hammer and chisel, they're on for a while.
> All I can say is… don't move! There is a
> snake by your foot!

> **BURT**
> That's a green snake and they won't hurt
> you. They eat bugs.

The silence from above was broken by the sounds of those flutes
playing off in the distance. As she looked up to see a squirrel race
through the tree tops away from the coming sound she says…

> **JANET**
> Oh crap, now what?

Burt rose to his feet; even the birds seem to follow the squirrel
to safety. Burt gritted his teeth…

> **BURT**
> (Angerly)
> What kind of religious nuts are these
> people? Are they some kind of cult hiding
> out here in the woods?

As she looked to the sound she said…

> **JANET**
> I don't think so. There are Aztec
> markings all around and as for hiding,
> they're not a secret cult. You found
> them! How did they build those buildings
> without being seen?

Burt pointed to the top of the wall and signaled her to come over
and he will give her a boost up. She stepped on his knee and placed
her hand on his shoulder. He then lifted her up to the top of the
wall and as she popped her head up over the top, holding on with both
hands, a gunshot rang out and a bullet shattered the concrete wall
right by her hand. She let go and fell on Burt.

As they lay there determining the damage of that idea, the sound of
flutes grew closer and closer, only this time mixed in are the
repeated squeaks of something turning. Burt signaled her to get
behind him.

As she slipped between the safety of the wall and Burt, she noticed he is sweating a lot. As the sound grew closer she tried to take his vitals…

JANET
You're burning up.

BURT
I don't think this is the time for that.
They're dragging something heavy this way
in some kind of a cart. You can hear the
weight grinding on the dry axle.

Sounds of something running around the perimeter of the pit stirred the leaves and then over the walls appeared first one, and then another, heads of the black pit-bulls. Tup-Con was first to be seen playing her flute with such joy and enthusiasm. Followed by Lee-Yaa and then there was the Lord. In unison they turned to face the pit and the girls stopped playing and slowly lowered their instruments and smiled down on their captives.

They stood, watching, enjoying the moment with smiles and there were red markings on their bodies, which were partially covered by new dresses.

JANET
(Whispered)
This is a ritual. This ain't good.

The Lord unfolded his arms and took one step forward and in a language that neither recognized; he spoke for several minutes. Still hiding behind his gold mask, he is holding a small golden scepter that he pointed to the heavens as he continued. Then he looked back down into the pit and said…

LORD
(Pointing off into the distance)
There! It is done, Christians! We will
test the strength of your god!

The sound of the squeaky wheel returned and two heads appeared over the wall pulling some cage on a wagon. They positioned the back of the cage to the edge of the wall where there was a cutout for the lower cart. The notch was made for the cart and by the scratches in the wall this was used before. Suddenly, the big head of a gator appeared and smiled down at them.

It snapped and lunged at the two men in camouflage and with such power it almost dumped the cage over. One on each side held the latches in their hands and as they looked over to Lord, they waited.

BURT
(Yelled)
You can't do this!!! This is murder!!!

Janet stepped out from behind him and yelled…

JANET
I am not a Christian!!! I am not one of
them!!!

This turned the Lord's head, just a little, but she noticed it.

TUP-CON
(Smiling)
Then you need not worry, for this one only
eats Christians.

Burt stepped forward, and said in a smart-ass tone…

BURT
I thought we were to be fed to the lions!

Rage came over the Lord's face that could only be seen in his eyes,
but he did not reveal it in his voice…

LORD
If I had one, I would be glad to provide
it for you, but I prefer a slower death.
So now is the time to pray to your god,
Christian.

With that said he pointed his scepter at the cage and it was lowered
into the pit. The sound of two claps, snap and the door fell open.
Burt pushed Janet behind him and grabbed a table leg from the floor.
It was full of deep scratches, as such a tool it must have been used
before.

Out popped the head of the gator and it plunged to the floor and landed
in the small puddle of water. With lightning speed it whipped around
and with its powerful tail, it flung trash and broken furniture across
the pit floor. Opening its large jaws with one powerful hiss… it
revealed their future.

Lord raised his scepter and the two men raised and closed the door
latching it in place. He then snapped his fingers and the flute
playing began as they all turned and walked away. The standoff
began.

DISOLVE TO:

INT. THE PIT — AFTERNOON

Over the last six hours they had tossed whatever they could get their
hands on, to keep him back. For a time, he slipped back into the
safety of the puddle, but slowly returned. His eyes were never

removed from his dinner. This time he meant it. He was not backing off and he raced at the two of them.

                              JANET
                         (Yelled)
                    Shove it down his throat!!!

Burt did just that. The gator snapped the leg in half and backed away spitting out the broken bits of wood, covered in blood. As he retreated to the cover of the puddle and its cooling properties, the waiting game continued.
                              BURT
                    Well that was a good idea and bought us some
                    time. But he is not going away and I don't
                    see another table leg to feed him.

They scoured the pit with their eyes trying to find some way to defend themselves from this relentless killer. Burt spotted a short piece of galvanized water pipe sticking out of the wall. After some persuading, he was able to break it loose. It was only two feet of pipe, but it was something hard that they could use for defense. He scraped it on the floor trying to sharpen one edge and make threatening sounds.

CUT TO:

INT. THE PIT - NIGHT

Minutes turned into hours and the heat of the day gave way to an afternoon shower. It poured for over an hour and at first the water was welcomed, for they could get a drink and she could wash the brown goo out of her hair. Then the rain started to form pools and the pit started to fill expanding the puddle. Both of them moved to the remaining high ground.

Their new companion sank into deeper water, hardly moving and never taking his eyes from them. He seemed to have taken naps all day, so he was rested for the night. Burt moved them to the corner even though it was in six inches of water. He had her sit behind him and he pressed her into the corner to protect her. He pulled his legs in tightly and she did the same.

The dreaded darkness of the night had started to come as another storm approached. It rained for another hour and then moved on. They heard their friend moving off to the other side, still holding his ground. The water had crept up another two inches, making him lighter and quicker as he tested his tail on the floating trash. The waves lapped on her legs as he grew closer in the dark. Finally, the moon lit part of the pit and the sounds of water splashing got closer. Burt hit the wall with the pipe several times and growled at the beast. The water stilled and silence filled the air as they waited.

BURT

If I fall asleep, wake me.

JANET

And just tell me how you can sleep?

BURT

It will happen. All we can do is talk to
keep each other awake.

They talked for hours. Burt was 47 and five years from retiring.
He had heard there were drug dealers in these parts and wanted to
check it out. He had met Janet at the hospital and invited her along
as cover, never dreaming this was here.

Burt had seen the scars on her body and tried several times to get
her to talk about it. Exhausted and trying to do everything she could
to stay awake, she told him her story. Leaning her head on his
shoulder trying to stay awake, memories came back from her tortured
past.

JANET

I always trusted cops. They told me I was
walking down the street one cold day when
a cop spotted me and knew something was
wrong. I guess I was wearing rags and had
no shoes on. It was a winter day and that
is why he stopped. My mother kept me in
the basement and I never saw the light of
day until that very day.

Janet rubbed her right arm where the scars from her mother dumping
boiling water on her still showed.

JANET

They think I was seven at the time. I had
no emotion, so they told me. I don't
remember much other than the pain she would
inflict on me. Then she would leave me in
the dark most of the time. Because I was
still growing, I convinced her to loosen
the chain on my ankle. That day I pulled
with all of my might and slipped my foot
out. I was free for the first time.

Janet had been told that it would help to tell people about what had
happened, but if she opened up to anyone, they would just pull away.
Burt noticed she was starting to refer to herself as ***a third party***.

JANET

I remember she would bring her boyfriends
down to her and they would rape the (more)

little girl that was me. She told the
little girl, she liked to watch.

Rubbing her right shoulder she continued…

                    JANET
          The doctors told me I had one hundred and
          seventeen scars. From cigarettes, to
          bite marks, to whippings with electrical
          cords. They gave her to a nice family that
          tried to give the girl… me, love and show
          me how to return it, but it is hard for me.
          I guess it was too much, for too long. I
          have had a lot of surgeries to remove the
          scars, but the ones inside I will always
          carry.

She leaned her head on his.
                    JANET
          I keep them in a box in my head. The box
          holds the black oozing bag of bad memories.
          I got married once, but he could not handle
          me and my box. He would get drunk and the
          beatings would start all over again. My
          coworkers saw all the bruises he put on me,
          so that was the last of him. I hope there
          is room for all of this new stuff in that
          box.

Neither Burt nor Janet knew that one of the guards was silently
standing just over their heads. He had heard the whole conversation,
until they fell asleep.

DISSOLVE TO:

INT. THE PIT - NIGHT

Burt was awakened to the thrashing of water as the great beast raced
toward them. It grabbed hold of his arm and whipped him across the
room. His screams filled the black air and she stood pressing
herself tightly in the corner. The battle went on as he was being
flipped over and over. The sound of breaking bones echoed off the
walls and she could hold it in no more and let out a muffled scream.

Silence filled the pit as small sounds are made of trash moving and
scraping. Then there were no more sounds. She stood in the dark
trembling in fear saying…
                    JANET
          I don't want to die this way.

As Janet looked to the heavens she closed her eyes and waited. She slipped back into her room of safety that she had made in her mind. A place she had made as a child and closed the door behind her. There it was quiet, clean, and bright. Once more she was protected from evil. Only this room had new people that loved her.

A breeze crossed her face and she opened her eyes to see the darkness was slipping back into the cracks and was returning under the ground. She couldn't bear to look and kept her eyes to the sky.

JANET
> (Whispered)
> Let the sun come up quickly.

Still trying not to look, she squatted back down, leaning on the wall she thought…

JANET   V.O.
> *You should look, he may be alive and you*
> *can help.*

She moved her eyes to the other side of the pit scanning for Burt. It was still too dark to see but as she waited, the silhouette of the beast could be seen. Under him, mixed with the trash, one leg stuck up from the wet shallow grave.

Beast and woman sat and stared at each other until she could stand it no more, then she sat all the way back down into the pool. As the day wore on, he too moved, but all the time holding his bounty under the water, tenderizing the meat.

CUT TO:

INT.   THE PIT - DAY

The sun was straight up in the sky and the full heat of the day was cooking everything. The stench in the pit was stifling and it was hard to breathe for it was so still and dead. As she splashed water on herself to help keep cool, she could hear footsteps coming up, off in the distance.

Janet rose back to her feet and pulled herself tightly into the corner and waited. She had time to think and decided not to let them know she was afraid. Janet wiped the fear from her face and thought…

JANET
> (Whispered softly)
> I will not let them see fear in me. I will
> meet them head on, whatever death there is
> for me I will walk with my head up. I gave
> that to my mother and I will not give that
> to them.

Janet stepped out from the corner and stood in the center of the pit on the high ground. Placing her hands on her hips, looking up in the direction of the sound… she waited. It was one of the men in camouflage and he was startled to see her waiting for him. He stopped for a moment, then moved nearer the wall and reached down.

JANET

What's next?

The guard set his gun down resting it on the wall and used both hands to lift something. Janet did not move, she was sure this was her death he was lifting. Then over the wall it came, a rope ladder. He stood there looking at her, but she did not move, staring back at him defiantly. Behind her, she heard the sound of the beast moving, making a loud popping sound deep in its throat. She jumped only slightly, never taking her eyes off the guard. He pointed to the rope ladder and indicated for her to come up.

Janet slowly lowered her arms and walked toward the ladder, grabbing the rungs. Placing her right foot in the first rung, she briefly tried to figure out how to lift herself up without scraping the skin off her toes. Then a voice deep inside, yelled at herself…

JANET   V.O.

Move! Get out of here!

Step by step Janet made her way to the top. It was then she realized just how heavy her chains were, or maybe it was the lack of food. She reached out to the guard to help her and he took her hand. She put her left foot on the top of the wall and her right hand on his shoulder, it was then she noticed something. She stopped and looked hard at the man, he had no body odor, but yet he was wet.

She lifted his hand still holding hers and she looked at his arm. He motioned for her to move along. Dragging the last of her chain over the wall he let go and pointed down the path. She turned and tried to ask a question, but he pushed the barrel of the gun into her side and gently pushed her along. Without a sound she did as he directed, for she was joyous over surviving the pit.

Now she found herself walking across some type of brick road. Her chains clanked as they were drug over the bricks. Off in the distance, she could see the black pyramid between the tall trees. As they moved to the clearing, the hot sand was burning her feet. He pointed to six poles holding up a small covering and so she then quickened her pace to the cooler sand under the lean-to.

There he pointed to one of the poles that had a heavy chain bolted half way up from the earth. He pointed down then quickly up indicating she would need to lift it up and as she did, she revealed a metal collar. He pointed to her neck and wide eyed she complied.

JANET

Anything is better than what I just went
through.

Janet started to place the rusty collar around her neck, but he took
it and tried cleaning it on his pant leg first. It was a kind act
she thought, as he stepped in to gently press it closed then pulled
from his pocket a padlock to lock it shut. He then removed his
canteen to give her a drink and Janet gladly took several gulps.

JANET
(Smiles)

Thank you for your kindness.

Without saying a word he walked away. Janet sat down in the sand,
exhausted from all that she had been through. The sand on the collar
that he had missed and its weight was digging into her flesh, but
at this point she did not care. She had survived the pit and wondered
what was next as she watched the guard walk away.

She quickly looked around and saw that she was alone. It was then
she could take a good long look around. Each of the post of her new
confines had a collar with a chain. Only one was rubbed clean with
just the start of new rust. There was someone here just before her.
After about an hour she fell asleep in the heat of the day. A gentle
wind crossed over her.

END SCENE

EXT. LEAN-TO - EVENING

After several hours of badly needed sleep, Janet dreamed that it was her turn in the jaws of the gator. As he lunged at her, she let out a guttural muffled scream as though she were hit in the gut. She sat up and looked around. The heat of the day was gone, replaced by a nice breeze blowing off the water and she could smell food. As her eyes adjusted and focused, she spotted two bowls next to her, one with table scraps and one with warm water. There was no one around and at this point she did not care. She devoured the food and drank all the water.

                         JANET   V.O.
          I am nothing more than a dog to these
          people, whoever they are and I must show
          them I am a person like them.

Janet remembers the police training course on abductions she took a year ago.

                         JANET
                    (Whispers)
          Just survive. Show them you're a person
          with a home and a life.

Janet cleaned the food bowl with the beach sand and placed them both back near the end of the covering at the end of her chain. She then brushed the sand from under her collar and off her ankles from under her leg irons.

Checking over her body for cuts and infections, Janet determined she would heal. She tried not to think of the gator that ate her friend, as she tried to straighten her hair, still filled with dried clumps of trash from the pit.

The collar was made of heavy rusted steel with loops for the large brass lock and about six feet of rusted heavy log chain. The log chain was bolted half way up to one of the six posts holding up a simple wooden lean-to covering that provided shade. The tin cover was small in size, about six feet by eight feet, only about five feet high with palm fronds on top.

                         JANET
               Primitive, but moving up!

There were the same chains bolted in the same place on each other post. As she pulled each one of the ends of the chains up from under the sand, they had the same type of collar.

The first one closest to Janet had been there for some time. The second, the same thing covered with rust and difficult to move. However, the third showed signs of use, for it moved easy and had fresh rust. The part nearest to the skin was polished. As she sat there on her knees holding the collar in her hands, she rubbed the smooth inner lining, and then looked up at the pyramid thinking…

> **JANET**   V.O.
> *This was just polished with the skin of someone's neck. But what happened to this one?*

The sun was gone and only a soft glow filled the air, lighting her surroundings. Quickly she tried to draw a map in her head of the location of everything around her.

Leaning on the south side of the cover was a crudely made wall of wood laced together with vines. As she moved away from her post, stretching her chain so she could see behind it, she found a hill of sand that ran down to the woods. The cover and pyramid were on higher ground with woods on three sides.

She could hear the water lapping on the beach just beyond it. Down near the water was a small lagoon with two tall black towers and the boat dock she had walked on, a life time ago. There was no sign of Burt's boat.

Darkness was closing in as the moon shone through a large dead tree near the dock in front of the pyramid, down by the water. As she moved to the safety of the center of the cover, she curled up in a small ball trying to make the best of her new home.

The sand under her was still warm as the air from the night was cool with the sea breeze. Janet pushed the sand away making a small indentation to sleep in, to help keep away the cold.

> **JANET**
> (Whispers)
> I will survive this!

As visions of that dead tree came into her mind, its bleached white wood remaining as a testament of its once greatness, Janet declared…

> **JANET**
> I will not end up like you, Mr. Tree; I will use your strength.

She fell asleep.

DISOLVE TO:

EXT. THE LEAN-TO – MORNING

In Janet's exhaustion, she did not move the whole night dreaming of her safe place, while in the soft sand. That was not until she was awakened by a wet nose sniffing her ear. She sprung awake and rolled away from the intruder crashing into the wooden wall behind her, knocking it over.

As she sat at the end of her chain, she could see it was one of the two black dogs. Unaffected by her display of fear, one marked a post as the sound of two hand claps drew their attention. They returned in the direction of the water and disappeared in front of the pyramid.

She saw the sun was just starting to rise as she moved back to the comfort of her post. Trying to brush the sand from her eyes, she looked around and spotted something she had not seen before.

                         JANET
          Is it real?

Janet wondered out loud in a whisper, as she stared at the dead tree for a moment. The light slowly brought things into more clarity.

                         JANET
                   (Whisper's into her hand as she
               covered her mouth.)
          Oh my god, it's a person!

A woman dangled from the end of a rope, draped over a white branch of the bark less tree, she moaned in pain. Her hands and elbows were tied behind her as she dangled from her bound elbows.

As the light filled the air, she could see this woman was covered with cuts and sores. Her chained feet dangled just inches from the sand as she rocked on the end of her tether.

It was then Janet strained to see, rising up on her knees for a better cautious look.
                         JANET
                   (Whispers)
          What on earth? Her feet look like they are
          blue, and so are her hands. Has the blood
          been cut off for that long? They had
          better get her down from there or…

Janet sits back and says to herself…

                         JANET
          Say nothing, or you will be in that tree.

After some time, one of the men dressed in camouflage, walked over to stand beside the dangling woman. He smiled as he looked back at the pyramid and there was a small flash.

JANET

(Whispered)

They take a picture like she was bagged
prey. Am I looking at my future?

Then the two girls appeared. One of the girls was holding a small camera which she handed back to the man.

Both girls, wearing only the same black ankle bracelets that seems to have become part of their skin and big smiles, taunted the hanging girl, by poking her with sticks. She twitched to their joy as she begged for them to stop. It was then that Janet can see her face was also blue.

JANET

Paint… Some sort of ritual?

Suddenly there was the sound of two hand claps. The girls dropped the sticks, turned and ran toward the front of the pyramid, then hit the ground on their knees bowing. A man held out something and one of the girls took it as he pointed to the woman. The camouflaged guard stepped back to get a better look as the girls walked over to the hanging woman. Slowly one raised her hand, revealing a gun.

JANET

(Whispered)

She is going to kill her.

WOMAN

(Yells)

NO!

The gun fired, revealing it was a stun gun and both leads deliberately miss. As she twitched, struggling to get free, the two girls laughed and ran to get both leads. Each holding one, they looked her over to determine the best place to plant them, while dragging the points tortuously over her skin. The back of the pyramid was now open and they looked back to see a hand point down and heard him say…

MAN

She is a runner, get the feet.

The two girls smiled at each other and each grabbed a rusting end to her leg irons. As her raw feet were lifted, vines wrapped in her chains became visible. Each held on tightly to the chains on her shackled feet as she struggled and they slowly raised the hand holding the pronged end of the stun gun up. Then simultaneously, they jabbed them into the balls of her feet. The girl let out a scream.

They both backed away and Tup-Con laughed with such joy, as she held the gun in both hands.

TUP-CON

This is how we treat runners.

Tup-Con pulled the trigger and the first shock raced into the girl's body and she began twitching and screaming in pain. She must be today's fun. But Janet noticed there were only three of them. One of the guards was missing. They took turns passing it back and forth until the battery was dead. The hanging woman had passed out from the pain and was motionless. Two claps came from inside the pyramid and a hand pointed to the woman and the three jumped to his command.

She was lowered to the ground with a thud and dragged toward the cover. Backing up with fear, Janet pushed toward her post until her feet had dug ruts in the sand and she could push no more.

JANET
(Whispered)

Am I next?

They drug her in the sand to the west post, the one with the newly polished collar, and the guard pulled out another brass lock, they chained her collar in place, dropping her in the sand. They stood over her as she lay face down. From the back of the pyramid the two canines appear without a sound.

JANET
(Softly)
She will suffocate if you don't move her.

LEE-YAA
(Snaps)
You move her, you're the nurse!

The guard kneeled down to untie her arms. As he began to roll her over, Janet scooted closer and helped lift her head from the sand and slowly turned her over.
JANET
(Pleads)
I am going to need a first aid kit. There
are several deep cuts, embedded thorns and
here she has bites.

Two loud claps came from the pyramid and the two girls ran inside and dropped to their knees in the dark shadows of the doorway. The guard started to slip back into the woods, stopping only to recoil his line. As they talked, Janet checked where they had tied her hands and elbows. While she checked her pulse and eyes, she tried to understand what the blue was made of. For it did not rub off, but seemed to wear off with time, like a dye. The soles of her feet and the palms of her hands were turning pink, so it must come off.

The nurse in Janet dragged the woman further under the cover to examine her better and discovered she was covered in deep cuts, bites and palm frond thorns are stuck in her feet. She removed the taser wires and the woman showed signs of life with a small moan of pain.

                         JANET
               That's a good sign.

Lee-Yaa returned with a first aid kit, threw it in the sand and walked back the way she came.
                         JANET
               Thank you.

She flipped the kit over and noticed the name of Burt's boat on it. As she was checking and cleaning the woman's wounds she had some time to think…
                         JANET   V.O.
                    The two girls are sadistic and one of the
                    guards is the same, but the one that helped
                    me out of the pit seemed to be kinder.

Suddenly two shadows appear behind Janet and one spoke.

                        TUP-CON
               He wants to see you.

She turned to face them and saw that Tup-Con and Lee-Yaa were both dressed in black. Tup-Con bent down to unlock Janet's collar…

                        TUP-CON
               You do just what I say.   Do you understand?

                         JANET
               Yes.

Each grabbed an arm and she rose to her feet.

                        LEE-YAA
                    (Softly)
                    We are going in the front. You are not to
                    speak unless he speaks to you and asks you
                    a question. You will immediately drop to
                    your knees in his presence and bow your
                    head in respect. Do not look upon the
                    body. Do not look into his eyes.

They walked her to the water's edge.

                        LEE-YAA
               Clean yourself!

Janet happily complied. As she stepped in, the warm salt water felt good on her skin. There, on the dock, is a bar of soap and a towel, but first she slowly moved in up to her waist rubbing the water on her skin removing the memories of the pit. Janet then lowered her head under water to try to soak out the dried bits of food from her hair. After a good soaping and some work she looked and felt better.

Standing on the dock staring out to sea, with the warm sun and sea breeze to help dry her, she thought of better times, and for a moment forgot what lay before her and that her feet were chained. That moment ended quickly as Lee-Yaa was now standing behind her touching her blond hair admiringly…

JANET
You look fine, it's time.

For the first time, Janet sensed Lee-Yaa seemed to be the nicer of the two. As they neared the open front door, Tup-Con grabs her by her hair and pulls her head back with a snap.

TUP-CON
If I see you ever look up at him, I will
gouge your eyes from your head with my bare
hands! Do you understand?

JANET
Yes! I will not ever look at him!

Two claps came from inside and they moved silently in. Janet's chains started to drag on the floor, so Lee-Yaa snapped at her…

LEE-Yaa
Pick up your chains!

Janet complied. They turned in unison, bent down, walking in quickly and all got on their knees. Tup-Con on one arm and Lee-Yaa on the other, held Janet's face to the floor.

No one said a word as they waited. The shackle was pressing deeply into the skin of one of her ankles and as she tried to adjust it, she was pushed further into the floor. As they waited, she noticed how clean and cool it feels inside with her face pressed firmly to the floor.

JANET   V.O.
They have air conditioning, but I saw no
wires.

There was movement in front of her and she could hear him shift on his throne. In a very high pitched tone, Lord spoke…

LORD
Is it true you are trained as a nurse?

                              JANET
                    Yes, My Lord.

Lord liked that, she knew her place. Both Tup-Con and Lee-Yaa
loosened their tight grip on Janet's arms as reward for respect.

                              LORD
                    Lee-Yaa was trained in medications in our
                    country, but you have more experience, I
                    feel.

Silence once more filled the room as she was sure her ankle must be
bleeding by now.
                              LORD
                    I am going to entrust you two with her care.

Both girls twitched with this news and pushed their nails into the
flesh of both Janet's arms. She gasped softly in pain as she is
pressed further into the floor.
                              LORD
                    They will give you what you need.

No one moved as the Lord shifted once more on his throne. He was
looking at two bites on his body. One was on his arm and the other
on his leg. After a minute he spoke…

                              LORD
                    I awoke with these two bites yesterday.
                    They seem to be getting worse. I have
                    taken some antibiotics, but they don't
                    seem to be working.

                              JANET
                    (Spoke with power in her voice.)
                    I would have to look upon the body and I
                    cannot do it from the floor. I would need
                    your permission, my Lord.

Five nails dug deeper into her flesh from both sides.

                              LORD
                    It is granted, let her up.

The weight of the two girls lifted off her arms and slowly blood
started to return to her appendages as she got herself back up
straight.

For a moment she rubbed her ankle and saw it was fine. Without taking
her eyes off the floor she approached the Lord, still holding onto
her chains. With the girls on both sides they guide her to his side.
She slowly stared at his foot, then his ankle, then his leg. There

was a badly infected open sore. He held down his arm and she saw
another, not quite as bad.

Janet reached up her free hand and with one finger points to the leg.
Then realizing she had power, returned to her position of respect
on the floor next to the Lord.

                         JANET
              It is badly infected and will require
              cleaning before it will heal. It looks
              like a recluse spider bite.

                         TUP-CON
              (Heroically)
              It was a brown spider, with a small body
              and thin legs. I smashed it. We keep it
              very clean here.

Sensing fear in Tup-Con's voice…

                         JANET
              (Reassuringly)
              I can see you take great care. They can
              be brought in packages or come in on their
              own. They like cool dark places.

The Lord clearly in pain spoke softly…

                         LORD
              What recommendations do you make?

                         JANET
              You should go to a hospital for treatment.
              If that is not possible, the wound must be
              cleaned to remove the poison.   If
              untreated, the poison or the infection
              could kill you.

Both Tup-Con and Lee-Yaa returned to the floor with Janet, where all
awaited his response.
                         LORD
              You will do this. You two are to give her
              whatever she requests.

                         JANET
              Now? Here?
                         LORD
              Yes.

                         JANET
              I would need to examine you more (more)

closely and for that, I would need to look
on the body and look into your eyes.

Tup-Con twitched at the thought.

                         LORD
          Granted, now tell them what you need.

Starting to rise, Janet looked at Tup-Con, then Lee-Yaa, who now have
anger in their eyes.

                        JANET
          I will need to clean my hands with soap and
          clean water… not salt water. I'll also
          need knives, alcohol, clean towels, and
          six feet of rope.

The Lord looked at Tup-Con and pointed to the back room with his eyes.
Both girls ran to get her request. The Lord was in pain as he
stretched out his leg, but did not say a word of it.

                         LORD
          There is soap and water in the back. You
          may clean yourself in there.

Janet rose to her feet, still holding onto her chain, as she quickly
walked to the back, head down. There in the back room was a sink
with all the items she had requested laying on the counter. Tup-Con
on one side and Lee-Yaa on the other, both glaring.

As Janet approached the sink…

                        JANET
                 (Talking to Lee-Yaa)
          Tie one end of the rope around your waist
          and the other to the middle of my chain to
          keep them off the floor.

She complied and Janet started to clean her hands.

                       TUP-CON
                 (Whispering into Jan's ear)
          If you kill him, you will wish you died
          instead.

Janet said nothing at first then said…

                        JANET
          You both may have killed him already by
          taking so long to get him help.

Tup-Con's eyes widened as she saw Janet's fate become hers.

> **JANET**
> This is going to be bad. Do you have any
> morphine for the pain?

> **TUP-CON**
> No. He would not take it if we did.

They returned to treat his wounds, this time Janet checked his pulse
and looked closer at the bites. His body was hairless, slim and next
to no fat. His legs and arms were hard to the touch from his strong
muscles.

> **JANET**
> You are running a fever from the infection.

She felt his forehead with her hand, as she looked into his eyes for
the first time.

> **JANET**
> I think we have gotten it just in time.
> You are lucky to have these two that serve
> you so well. The dead skin must be
> removed, then cleaned and to do that I must
> scrape it away. This will hurt! Do you
> want anything for the pain?

> **LORD**
> Your touch is very gentle, I will need no
> drugs. You do what you must to return
> health to the body.

She began… The Lord showed no reaction to the pain he was in as she
scraped clean both wounds draining out all the infection she could.
Covering them with a cream and then gauze, she taped them in place.

> **JANET**
> Reapply the cream and change the gauze
> twice a day, and be sure to take the
> antibiotics.

When finished, Janet placed some anti-biotic cream, gauze, band aids,
aspirin, some pain meds and syringes in a towel to take with her.
She thought that she may need them for the girl at the lean-to.
Tup-Con and Lee-Yaa returned to the floor pushing Janet down with
them.

There they waited for the Lord to dismiss them, but there was only
more silence as they all lay there bowed and kneeled on the floor.

The silence was broken with the ringing of a phone but still no one
moved. Then he snapped his fingers and the two jumped up pulling
Janet to her feet and they all backed out the door. Tup-Con leaned
over to Lee-Yaa…

>   **TUP-CON**
> You take her and I will get the phone.

Lee-Yaa and Janet quickly returned to the lean-to cover and Janet picked up her collar and placed it around her neck in compliance. Lee-Yaa studied her for a moment then gently placed the lock in her collar. She continued to study Janet for a moment then with a glare coming from her jet black eyes, she backed away.

Voices were coming from out of the back of the pyramid. It was Tup-Con telling someone to hold on. Then the Lord speaks in a new voice…

>   **LORD**
> Do you have the new shafts done yet? We
> will need them this week. I am sure under
> normal usage the old design would be fine,
> but I wanted to test it for the maximum load
> it could produce using this system and it
> twisted like it were made of clay.

By now the woman next to Janet had returned to consciousness. She was only pretending to be out when they first returned. Her frightened eyes revealing her thoughts…

>   **YOUNG WOMAN**
> You are brave to speak to them that way.
> They will kill for any reason.

>   **JANET**
> Not me. They need me. Now let's start
> with names. I am Janet. What is your
> name?
>   **CAT**
> Catena, but people call me Cat.

>   **JANET**
> I like that name. And are you allergic to
> any drugs?
>   **CAT**
> No.

The Lord's voice could once more be heard.

>   **LORD**
> Yes, yes, the power is fivefold stronger
> than originally estimated, evidenced by
> the condition of the shaft. I am going to
> send it to you. Yes, I would like that,
> but it can't be for several weeks now. I
> am going to be out of the area then.

DISOLVE TO:

EXT.   LEAN-TO – MID-MORNING

A brief shower appeared once more over them, as Janet pulled out more
of Cat's thorns and re-cleaned the cuts and placed a new band aid
over each one. Janet then took the syringe and gave her a shot as
she explained what she is doing like a teaching nurse. Then Jan
looked closely at the blue on Cat's hands and feet and asked…

> **JANET**
> What is this? It's not paint, but
> something in the skin like a dye of some
> type. What does it mean?

Cat stared off into the woods.

> **CAT**
> You will find out in time when it is your
> turn.

Then she closed her eyes in pain of the memory. The kit was returned
to a place of safety and they both retreated to the shade under the
cover as the sun returned. Cat told how she was lost on back roads
and ended up walking.

> **CAT**
> I walked up to the Bates Motel, got a dart
> in my back and ended up in this place.
> They call us Gifts, you know. We just fell
> into their trap. There is no one to stop
> them. After time, they trusted me and I
> started to clean and cook for them. When
> I had a chance to run, I did. But I just
> got lost until he found me. I could not
> have survived much longer and I chose to
> swim to my death. But I failed at that,
> you should just let me die.

> **JANET**
> (Smiling)
> I can't let you die, that is not a part of
> what I have become.

Janet looked to the sea in a long stare…

> **JANET**
> I have lived through worse and I will live
> through this.

Then, turning back to Cat and smiled reassuringly.

> **JANET**
> We will survive this, you will see.

Cat rubbed her legs and feet.

>   **CAT**
>   Do you think I will ever get feeling back?
>   I can't even move my toes.

>   **JANET**
>   You may have nerve damage, but with time
>   I think you will be fine.

They talked for hours until Tup-Con headed into the woods carrying
something and Lee-Yaa came with two bowls; one of food and one of
water. They shared the scraps, but it had been days without food
for Cat. So at breakneck speed, she ate most of the food, and then
apologized. Janet proceeded to clean the bowls with sand and set
them in the sun.

>   **CAT**
>   Why are you doing that? They treat us like
>   dogs! I just toss them back into the dirt.
>   Let them clean it up.

Janet moved in closer to Cat to whisper…

>   **JANET**
>   Let's see now. I found you hanging from
>   a dead tree and you watched me give one of
>   them orders.
>   (Tapping her chin)
>   Now who's way is better for survival?

END SCENE

EXT.   LEAN-TO - DAY

The sun was straight up above them and the heat of the day was suppressing. The heat and nourishment are ingredients for sleep so both napped to pass the time. By that afternoon, the sun shone very brightly on Cat's side of the cover, but still she slept.

Janet checked her patient and discovered fire ants on her legs and feet. She raced to kill them with her hands and woke Cat. The two of them, in a panic killed hundreds of the ants. The ants seemed to be everywhere as they tossed sand away from them in all directions. Finally, they retreated and surveyed the damage. Janet could see Cat was falling apart.

> **JANET**
> It will be ok Cat, try to hang on. They're gone now.

> **CAT**
> You don't understand. They will be back. They always come back, like them.

Cat glared at the woods with her eyes. She looked hard at Janet as her eyes filled with tears.

> **CAT**
> I don't know how much more of this I can take. I miss my home and my family.

> **JANET**
> Don't worry. We will be fine.

> **CAT**
> I used to think that, when I was like you, here for just a few days. But it has been months now and I think I am pregnant. When it's your turn, don't fight them like I did. They seem to enjoy it more.

Janet leans back on her post.

> **JANET**
> Do they all join in?

Flashes of the past begin to race through Janet's mind.

> **CAT**
> That is the weird part. It's always the same man. The others just stand and watch. I tried to fight him by hitting him and finally he got tired of it and pulled me by my feet until I was straight out tight by this collar. Then he stood on the chains attached to my feet and watched me struggle for air. Once I stopped, (more)

he pulled down his pants and loosened the
tension on the chains. Sometimes he would
come three times a day.

I just let him do his thing and I
waited for my moment to run. I tried to
swim, but the chains just pulled me under.
I had to walk back on the bottom to get air.
Oh by the way, the water is full of sharks.
I tried walking head high for a while and
one time I was bumped. So don't try the
water.

JANET
(Puzzled)

Bumped?

CAT
Yeah, a shark will bump you sometimes
before they attack. So the water is not
the way out.

It was then Cat spotted movement in the woods by the dead tree. She
recoiled pushing back to her post as she stared, her fists slowly
clinched. Janet could see it was the two guards watching them. They
both used a ladle to scoop water from a covered drum and then pour
it over their heads.

As each filled their canteens, one started to approach. He slowly
walked to Janet's side and stood next to her handing her his canteen.
As she looked up at him, he indicated she should take it and have
a drink.

It was an act of kindness and Janet quickly thanked him and drank
her fill. He then reached in his pocket and removed a napkin with
half a sandwich, handing it to Janet. She graciously took it and
looked up at her new friend…

JANET
(Tearing the sandwich in half)
But this is your food, you must eat too.

For the first time Janet heard him speak with a soft gentle voice.
He had a nice smile with kindness in his eyes. Janet knew firsthand,
how to survive and kindness was the way out. Any kindness meant they
knew she was a real person.

GUARD
It is too hot to eat and I saw that one eat
all the food.

Before Janet could say another word he walked away. She softly
thanked him again.

After eating Janet folded the napkin and placed it in the bowls. Then
thinking it might get him in trouble, she retrieved it and buried

it in the sand behind her.

Off in the distance an afternoon storm was rumbling. Janet's attention was drawn to the sky as flocks of seagulls were moving to the trees. Brown pelicans cooled themselves on the dock with their bellies full of fish. A school of blue spotted dolphins popped up for air and slipped back under the sea. A burst of cool air raced over them and off in the distance she could see a large ship moving by.

> **JANET**
> We must be near some type of sea port.

Cat squints her eyes to see…

> **CAT**
> I was hoping to walk to them, but never found them. When I waved at them, I was just too small for them to see me.

> **JANET**
> The storm is getting closer; it will be nice to have the cool rain.

Sand was blowing… The doors closed on the pyramid as the sky turned black with rain. Cat moved closer to Janet as a bolt of lightning hit the ground nearby and the thunder filled the air.

> **CAT**
> I am scared to death of these storms.

Janet still studying the sky spotted a wall of water coming at them…

> **JANET**
> Here it comes. Now we can get clean.

The rain started with ice cold water then small hail. Janet looked to the trees and the birds were hunkered down. She then checked on the pelicans and they had moved to a small sand bar that was found at low tide, where there were about twenty of them clustered together.

As she took it all in and the rain got heavier, she saw the pelicans turn to the storm's bounty and in unison they all opened their mouths and got a long drink of water from the sky. Janet then stepped out into the cool rain and did the same thing. Finding hail on their roof, she then popped it into her mouth like candy. Janet began scrubbing the dirt off of her body and out of her hair. She had learned to find joy wherever she could.

She saw streams of water pouring off the cover and she stood under them let them pour on her head and rinse off the last of the filth in her mind from the pit. As she scrubbed her head, she closed her eyes and remembered how the filth got there on that first night.

Another close clap of thunder made her jump and Cat let out a short scream.

> **CAT**
> Are you coming back?

Janet stayed to finish cleaning as best she could, as the rain started to let up. She noticed that puddles seemed to be all over. She looked at Cat under the cover and smiled, for it was a low spot that was ankle deep with water.

> **JANET**
> You had better get a drink while you can.

Cat just shook her head no. As quickly, as the storm started it ended, leaving the sound of dripping water all around with a soft cool breeze. It was the end of another day as the sun came out one more time to help dry things out before it set. As night started to come, bringing its dark fears, the other guard appeared and Cat recoiled in fear and disgust.

> **CAT**
> (Whispered)
> See, like the ants, he's back.

Janet stared at the man that Cat couldn't look at. He signaled her to come to him but she did not see. Now on his knees, he grabbed her leg iron chains and pulls on them as she retreated from his desires. Janet watched as he lowered his pants and moved closer.

> **JANET**
> Try to be careful, she may be pregnant with
> your child.

This news stunned him and he smiled back and then proceeded, but more gently. Off in the shadows Janet could see the other guard was watching. The next morning just before sunrise Janet heard a motor coming closer and closer.

> **JANET**
> (Softly, waking Cat)
> It's a boat. Could it be help? It's a boat
> coming closer and closer.

> **CAT**
> He is one of them; I think he brings the
> mail and supplies.

END SCENE

EXT.   LEAN-TO – EVENING (DAYS LATER)

Each day ran into the next as a routine seemed to take over until one afternoon the girls' shadows appeared over the napping Janet. Tup-Con kicked at her feet…

> TUP-CON
>> Wake up. Wake up.

Cat recoiled to her post knowing what was to come.

> TUP-CON
>> Get up. Get up.

Janet looked at them and then at Cat.

> CAT
>> (Softly)
>> It's your turn now.

Janet sat up and scooted over to the safety of her post, looking at both of the girls as her eyes adjusted to the bright sunlight. Tup-Con knelt down and removed the lock from her collar. Janet slowly opened her collar and felt just how heavy it really was. She laid it down in her lap and slowly closed it as her fingers ran over the smooth inner lining once covered with rust.

She held on to it realizing the safety it once offered as she faced the new unknown. She looked up at the girls, as she rubbed her fingers over her raw neck. Tup-Con got back up and snapped out…

> TUP-CON
>> Get up on your feet and come with us!

Lee-Yaa pulled at her hair…

> LEE-YAA
>> Now!

Janet crawled out and stood before them as both pointed to the water, her heart now raced as she wondered…

> JANET   V.O.
>> Is it my death I'm walking to, or the same
>> fate as Cat? I will not fight them.

Then, at the water's edge, Janet saw soap and a towel sitting on the dock. Tup-Con pointed and snapped…

> TUP-CON
>> You clean yourself!

JANET
(Smiling)

Gladly!

She saw how it took the wind out of Tup-Con's sails, and she thought…

JANET   V.O.
Now, I know what to do, verbal kung fu.

She remembered how a friend had taught her to let her boss yell all he wanted. Then just agree with him, regardless of what he said. It took all the fight out of them and they most times just walk away.

She stepped into the warm salt water and noticed two horse shoe crabs making love just under the dock.

JANET   V.O.
I bet you didn't get to take a bath first.

As she washed in the salt water she could hear some type of humming coming from the two black towers and tried to think what they must be for. There was a cable running from them to the pyramid.

Then she lost herself in the pleasure of washing with soap in warm water. The filth of days of sweat and dirt fell away, darkening the water at her feet. Then it flowed away, off into the vastness of the endless water.

She took her time and the girls let her. Once done she sat on the dock drying her blond hair and soaking her sore feet and ankles in the warm salt water. Another storm off in the distance blocked the sun and Janet realized another day was coming to an end and she was unsure of the future.

Tup-Con kept looking to the back side of the pyramid and finally got a signal from one of the guards.

TUP-CON
Come on, they're ready.

Janet's glistening soft blond hair blew in the afternoon breeze as her bright widening blue eyes looked up and she responded with a small knowing smile to her future. She rose to her feet and saw Cat leaning on her post with her legs drawn in and her arms holding them close to her. She slowly followed Tup-Con up the small incline, past the pyramid and looked at Cat as though it would help to see the future.

Walking up the incline she felt the chain digging into the soft sand making it harder to walk. The sand got between the shackles and her ankles and dug into her raw skin even more.
As they made the turn to the back, there in the center of the clearing,

the peak of the shadow of the pyramid was pointing at a small table or bench. It was the wall she knocked over, now sitting on three logs for legs to hold it up about a foot off the ground. There was a torch at each corner, not lit.

JANET

(Talking quietly to herself)

It must be a night thing.

Tup-Con walked over to it and pointed.

TUP-CON

Sit down.

As Janet approached, she placed the damp towel on the bench and sat down on it. The two girls now stood before her, the tip of the pyramid was now pointing between her legs, but she couldn't see their faces.

LEE-YA

The blood test is back and you are clean.
We are to prepare you for tonight.

JANET

Prepare me in what way?

Lee-Yaa leaned forward and grabbed her by her hair.

LEE-YAA

You will do what we tell you or we will tie you down and do it anyway.

JANET

(Smiled)

I only asked so that I may help you.

The two looked at each other…

LEE-YAA

We need you to move to the center for preparations.

JANET

Ok. May I move the towel so I have something soft to sit on?

She rose to her feet and did it anyway. She spread the towel out flat and then tried to move to the center. When her right ankle chain snagged on one of the beams, hanging up on the bench, she moved to fix it and bring all the chain up on the bench. The center of the chain shone in the sunlight as the point of the shadow moved closer, pointing out the coming of night and the darkness where evil resides.

She sat there brushing the sand from under her shackles and off her feet, where the water made it stick. Tup-Con pointed to the pyramid and Lee-Yaa smiled and walked toward it. The shadow now up to Jan's face, she could now see. She looked up to Tup-Con and saw just how young she was. Her brown skin glistened in the evening sun as she lifted her left foot and placed it on the bench next to Janet. Holding onto one of the poles, she looked back to the pyramid. Janet studied her black anklet that was about two inches wide and asked…

> **JANET**
>
> Is it made of leather?

Tup-Con was surprised and turned quickly to look at her.

> **TUP-CON**
>
> You act strangely for someone in your position.
>
> **JANET**
>
> What will be done to me, will not change who I am. May I touch it?

The girl moved her leg closer and arched her foot so Janet could see. It was soft to the touch and covered in fur. It seemed to be seamless and tight to her skin.

> **JANET**
>
> Clearly, it was removed from an animal that was just skinned. You must have put it on when it was still soft during another ritual, most likely.

She watched Lee-Yaa return and studied the same ankle band.

> **JANET**
>
> What does it mean?

Tup-Con touched the band with much pride.

> **TUP-CON**
>
> This is part of a young deer, its spirit lives on in me, giving me its strength and power to be quick and strong for my Lord. It is a rite of passing from childhood to woman guardian.

She was holding two small handmade jars covered in hieroglyphics.

> **JANET**
>
> Incan… Is this Incan writing? Can you tell me what it means?

The two looked at each other with puzzlement and Tup-Con responded…

TUP-CON

I see no harm in me telling you. It is a rite of cleansing for those who are unclean. Also this will bring your sexual desires to the surface as it does to the birds.

JANET

(Puzzled)

Birds?

TUP-CON

Yes, they are best known as the Blue-footed Booby and at mating season their feet turn bright blue indicating peak mating time. I think the color is very sexy don't you? And it goes so well with your white skin and blond hair. It's a perfect match to your eyes.

Janet was more at peace now and began to relax more.

TUP-CON

You are to be cleaned and prepared for tonight. You are a gift to us from the gods and we must prepare you for what you were sent to us for.

JANET

Will it hurt?

They both laughed.

TUP-CON

Well it may hurt in a good way, but this part won't.

Lee-Yaa set the jar at her feet and gently took one foot and stretched her leg out straight before her so it hung just over the edge. She tried to move the shackle further up her leg out of her way and Janet helped, still brushing the sand out of the way. Reaching in the jar the girl removed a small stick with hair tied to it making a small brush. Dripping from its end is dye the color of bright blue. Lee-Yaa slowly spread it on Janet's foot and Janet smiled.

JANET

It tickles. What is it for? I mean, why blue and why the feet?

Tup-Con and Lee-Yaa smiled at each other. Then Lee-Yaa told her the meaning.

LEE-YAA

The blue is for the sky and the sea. They are always clean and renewing... life (more) giving. We are to cover the feet.

As Lee-Yaa finished, she handed the brush to Tup-Con and she moved
to the left foot and they proceeded.

                         LEE-YA
               And in this way the past that you walked
               is cleaned. You are renewed for your next
               life here with us and the new life you will
               bring.

Janet sat back leaning on her hands, as now both her feet hung over
the end of the bench.   She was impressed by how gentle they were being
to her.
                         JANET
               You mean a baby, life giving, you mean I
               am to have a baby?

Lee-Yaa scratched her head and Tup-Con continued…

                         TUP-CON
               Well that would be nice, we like babies.
               But what she means is, your new life, with
               us, baby or not and what it will bring.

Janet sat up so Lee-Yaa could cover her hands and thinks…

                         JANET   V.O.
               A new life, I can't say I was doing much
               with the old one. I have always wanted
               kids, just could not find Mr. Right.
               Maybe I need to be like the crab and accept
               what comes. I am not getting any younger
               and it has been a long time between men.

Lee-Yaa finished both Janet's hands, also in bright blue saying…

                         LEE-YAA
               Now everything you touch will be with new
               power from the new you.

Then she gently pushed Janet back to lie down and brushed her hair
from her face.
                         JANET
               I understand the hands and feet, but why
               the face?
                         LEE-YAA
               Same thing, everywhere you have looked and
               those that look upon you will be gone and
               in your past life. You are free of it and
               will join us in a new and better life.

Lee-Yaa sat down and tilted her head.

LEE-YAA
You are not like the others. You are not afraid. I have never understood you white women. You don't seem to like sex and this is a special gift we give to you. We are saving you! You do not seem to understand, you are a gift from the gods and we give this to you in respect to them and to help you in the passing. Few ever receive such a chance to be reborn, you are very lucky.

Janet leaned her head back flat on the bench as Lee-Yaa gently covered her face in blue.

JANET
Well I would be lying if I said I was not afraid. I guess I still don't understand completely.

Tup-Con twisted the pole she was leaning on.

TUP-CON
We are saving you from your old life. All the evil that was around you will be replaced with people that really care for you. This is a great moment for you.

Janet thought some more then asked…

JANET
If I am to become one of you, then I must learn. What about you two, will you be bringing new life here with us?

They both looked at each other and laughed.

TUP-CON
Don't be foolish, how can we do that? We are Villkabomaba's.

JANET
What does that mean?

TUP-CON & LEE-YAA
We are Virgin's of the Sun.

JANET
(Looking at the pyramid)
Please don't get mad at me, but don't(more)

you sleep with him?

Lee-Yaa looked at Tup-Con who answered...

TUP-CON

It is ok that you don't understand. We are chosen to care for and to fill the body's needs for our Lord. He is in the body of a normal man and we help him. You do not understand that he too is a virgin.

Lee-Yaa smiled at her work.

LEE-YAA
(Looking at Cat)
We have trained for this all of our lives. To fail would bring great shame upon our families. He would return us in chains and throw us at our parents' feet in front of the whole town. I would rather drown like that one. She thought she could swim in chains, the poor little rich girl. I am sickened by her tears and take much joy in her pain.

JANET

You saw her?

Lee-Yaa looks to the woods.

LEE-YAA

Yes, there are cameras everywhere. We let her starve in the woods for a few days.

Off in the distant woods, Janet could hear footsteps in the leaves and all eyes turned to the sound. The sun was setting by now and Lee-Yaa rose to her feet.

LEE-YA

See what a nice job I did, the gods will be very proud.

Tup-Con stepped over to look and smiled...

TUP-CON

Yes, she did well for you.

JANET

Thank you, thank you both for talking to me. It helps a lot to just understand.

Janet lay there staring up at the first star of the night as a cool breeze blew through the trees and over her body. She raised her hands up so she could see and whispered...

JANET

(Whispered)

Everything I touch will be by a new person.
My past is gone.

Wiggling her toes she smiled, and looked up at Lee-Yaa.

JANET

Did you get everywhere?

LEE-YAA

(Smiled)

Yes. Soon your past will be over and all
behind you.

Janet lifted herself up to her elbows and looked off to the woods.
Two men stood there in the shadows next to the large drum one lifted
the lid as the other took out a ladle of water and poured it over
his head, then the other did the same. Janet could remember seeing
other drums like that one before, by the pit and the man without sweat
was wet on the back.

END SCENE

EXT. THE PYRAMID - NIGHT

The back of the pyramid slowly and silently opened to the darkness.
The girls came back out with two torches and lit them. They slowly
walked over and lit the four next to Janet, illuminating her for all
to see. They then drove the ends of the torches into the ground.

It was then that Tup-Con picked up the second jar left on the bench
at Janet's feet and held it up to the sky, whispering some symbolic
words to the heavens, then handed it to Janet.

> **TUP-CON**
> (Softly)
> Take a drink of this.

Janet held the jar in both hands, for it looked old and slowly brought
it to her lips as she smelled the liquid in it.

> **TUP-CON**
> It's not poison, it will help break down
> walls that stand in your way.

Janet took a drink. It was hard to swallow, because it was mostly
alcohol. She could feel it burn as it went into her stomach and it
quickly started to flow into her blood stream. With her eyes closed
she felt it pump down into her legs and back up into her chest and
finally into her mind and she relaxed. She opened her eyes and handed
it back to Tup-Con.

> **TUP-CON**
> Drink some more, it will help with your
> passing and remove the evil from your past
> so you only bring the good that is within
> you.
> (Said proudly)
> We make it ourselves from plants only found
> in land near the gods. It's very special
> and very powerful, because it comes from
> the gods.

Wanting this very much, Janet took another drink and then another.

> **JANET**
> I can take no more.

It was then that Janet realized that the drink is a home brew, like
white lightning and with the same punch.

Tup-Con then pulled a ribbon of leather from her golden vest and
looked at Janet. She moved closer to Janet and whispered…

> **TUP-CON**

(Whispered)
You must wear this when he comes out. Do
not remove it.

Tup-con then placed it over Janet's eyes and tied it gently in the
back.

Lee-Yaa had moved over to Cat and did the same thing then covered
Cat's eyes. Tup-Con and Lee-Yaa returned to the doorway, torches
in hand and waited. They then jabbed them into the sand in front
of the door and began playing their flutes. It was a different song
than before. The flutes got closer until they were on each side of
her. Then they stopped.

After another long pause, our Lord, dressed in his finest gold
apparel, prepared to speak to the gods in a different language. He
spoke words that Janet did not know.

LORD
We are grateful for your gift to us.
We are happy to help save her from a wasted
life. We have prepared her in the ways of
the past to cleanse her for the future.
Wherever she has stepped, is now in her
past life, whatever she has touched, is now
in her past life, wherever she looked and
who ever looked upon her, is now in the past
life.
We have brought the special ones here
this day for you and to be part of her
future. From the past that is saved, this
one will build on the future. From this
moment forward, you are new, reborn and
every step you take, hand you touch and
person you see will be guided by Ayar and
the family of our sun god.

Janet could feel the presence of other people all around her, helping
her and guiding her there in the silence. There were children
standing next to her and the presence of old ones looking down on
her. Their presence was there to guide her as they did the children.
She didn't move but thought…

JANET   V.O.
*It must be the drink, but I like the thought
of help and guidance.*

She relaxed even more, as her whole body began to tingle.

JANET

V.O.

> (Smiled)
> *Were there drugs mixed in with her drink?*
> *No they would not do that, drugs don't come*
> *from the gods.*

The Lord then slowly backed away and returned to his place. Janet could hear movement and noticed Lee-Yaa stood next to her. Lee-Yaa leaned over and softly touched Janet's head as she started to untie the knot to her blindfold. Janet jumped and let out a short light scream.

LEE-YAA

> (Whispered)
> You can remove your blind now, if you wish.

Lee-Yaa backed away. There before Janet stood the man that helped her out of the pit, the one that also gave her food and had been so kind to her. He was naked and the girls were wiping him down with water. He moved closer to the light and Janet could see he had no hair on his body and little body fat. His skin was such an odd color in the dim light, it seemed to glow. It was clear he was glad to see her. He smiled and stood before her as they looked into each other's eyes.

Tup-Con picked up the jar with the juice of the gods and said the same thing to him that she had said to her then handed it to him and he took a drink. Both girls stepped to her side.

LEE-YAA

> (Whispered softly)
> He is the nicest one here. You are lucky
> and don't even know it. The gods have
> brought you two together. He has waited
> all his life for you, as the gods told him
> of this day.

Janet's fears fell away and slipped back into the black cracks of her past where they belonged. He was shy and the girls coaxed him forward.

TUP-CON

> This is a very rare man; he is one that
> carries the seeds of our past. He is one
> of only six like him in the world. He
> holds our past in him and with the gods'
> help, those seeds will be passed on for you
> to carry and our future will have what he
> holds.

They helped him onto the platform as Janet leaned back, feeling the full effects of the drink. He hovered over Janet, as she gently ran her fingers up his arms, touching his skin for the second time. His arms were strong and he smiled. The girls helped as he lowered himself down onto Janet. A rush filled her body and she slowly embraced him and in moments began to show her enjoyment. Tup-Con looked down in puzzlement, then over at Lee-Yaa.

TUP-CON
(Puzzled)
Look at that. There is a white woman that likes sex!

Lee-Yaa stroked Janet's head and said…

LEE-YAA
You are our first.

Then she slowly poured cool water on his back.

When they finished they lay for a time enjoying the moment, then he stood before Janet and said…

GUARD
I hope you will be the first. Please try to have a water baby.

As he put on his clothes and headed back to his work, she thought about what he asked and signaled Lee-Yaa over to her side and asked…

JANET
What is a water baby?

Lee-Yaa looked surprised. So, Tup-Con softly told her…

TUP-CON
She is not from our home. Tell her.

LEE-YAA
(Looked over at him)
He is a water man. There are only six in the world that we know of. They are very special and can only be found in our land. They can be found nowhere else.
He came with us, because the gods spoke of this time through our Lord. Both men left their homes and families to come help in whatever was asked of them. You are the gifts they spoke of and the seed will be carried in you.

She leaned forward and whispered to Janet…

LEE-YA
If you have a water baby, you will become

> a much honored one. They have walked with
> our people for all time. Some say before
> the gods. They were sent here to prepare
> all of us, for the gods.

Only three burning torches remained at this point and Lee-Yaa joined Tup-Con in a whispered conversation by the pyramid. Two more torches started to flicker. Then a soft breeze put them out and only one remained behind Janet, casting a flicking glow down upon her new body and her new life. She remained sitting on the towel leaning back on her hands and watched the girls' attention turn to the Lord inside.

They disappeared inside as the last light went out. Janet remained motionless sitting in the same place.

> **JANET**   V.O.
> *They are not staying, no one is. Honored?*
> *Who would honor us here? Or back home?*
> *They're home!*

She pulled her legs up to her chest and wrapped her arms around them. In the soft moonlight she thought about her past life.

> **JANET**
> (Whispered)
> I have no one that cares about me. I am
> divorced and my last boyfriend cheated on
> me. I wanted a different life, and I got
> my wish.

Janet then looked at her blue hands and feet that were brighter in the moonlight she noticed that they seem to glow, or it was the drink and it was just in her mind. She rubbed her fingertips together and noticed that they still felt tingly. Looking up at the sky she reached down and touched her shackles and remembered she was still chained and then she started looking around. A stunned look came over her face as she realized that they left her all alone. She stared off into the distance towards the hypnotic sound of the waves.

> **JANET**
> (Whispers to herself)
> It must a sign of trust? No… they have
> cameras everywhere, but still it was a nice
> thing. They could have drug me back to my
> post and chained me back up like a dog and
> they didn't. It is a test.

It had been quite a day and Janet was starting to fall asleep.

JANET V.O.

> *Do I want to stay here or sleep in the soft*
> *sand? The pyramid is closed up and I am*
> *not going to sleep on these planks.*

Quietly, she lifted her chains off the wood and moved closer to the edge of the bench where she put her feet back down in the warm sand. Grabbing the towel she sat there for a moment enjoying the soft breeze blowing over her body moving her shoulder length hair over her skin.

Softly brushing the small of her back she felt the end of her blindfold. She pulled it out of her hair and gently wrapped it around her neck.

Janet was somehow keenly aware of her surroundings and spotted an owl quietly landing on the white branch of the dead tree. It turned its head from side to side, then without making a sound was gone. Everything seemed to glow in the moonlight.

Slowly, she rose to her feet, holding one of the torch poles for balance and as she straightened up to stand alone in the moonlight, the thought of a new life kept crossing her mind.

JANET

> (Whispered)
> I have had to start over before and try to
> rebuild but never was I a gift from the
> gods.

She walked to the sea and stood at the end of the dock enjoying her freedom from the past. The moonlight sparkled off the water as it lapped under her feet on the dock.

Alone in the dark and looking to the heavens, Janet reached out her arms, with her blue hands that seemed to glow even brighter opened and whispered…

JANET

> I am free of the past… guide me.

A sense of presence surrounded her as she felt every movement of her body was now controlled by others that loved her. Janet was at peace. The sea's gentle water crashing on the shore was hypnotically pulling at her and she stepped back to the safety of the cover by Cat. She made a pillow out of her towel and tried to take in all that had transpired. Looking off into the darkness of the woods she thought…

JANET V.O.

> *I no longer fear the darkness. I am*
> *surrounded by people that love me and will*
> *protect me. I do not know what is (more)*
> *before me, but somehow I am now empowered.*

The one word that kept returning in her mind was honored. She had
never felt honored before. She fell asleep quickly.

END SCENE

EXT.   LEAN-TO - MORNING

The sun brightened the sky and Janet woke with a smile. She looked down at her hands and feet and they were still bright blue.

JANET

> So, it wasn't a dream.

Sitting up and leaning on her pole, she rubbed her neck, realizing she was left unchained to her post. She then stretched out her still shackled legs and spread her toes apart admiring the fresh bright blue color. The words returned to her mind… *'Everywhere I step, everything I touch and everything I look upon is from a new person in a new life.'*

She smiled even bigger as she looked over to see Cat asleep, still wearing her blindfold.

Janet's eyes had started to adjust to the morning sun and she looked off into the woods and saw that both men had returned. Janet thought to nudge Cat and tell her that she could remove her blindfold now, but she let her sleep, so she wouldn't have to listen to her constant whining.

Cat awoke at the sound of the men coming and sat up. Once her blindfold was removed, she saw her tormentor standing over her; she recoiled, pushing herself tightly to her post so hard, she buried her feet into the sand. Once more he grabbed her shackles and pulled her out flat, he was to have his way.

Janet looked up to see a smile and a friendly hand extended. She took his hand and he helped her up to her feet. He handed her small wild flowers held together at the base with a blade of grass, used as string.

She took them gently from his hand and stared at them for a long time. Her mind raced back in time… she could not remember any man ever giving her flowers. Even for her wedding she had to buy her own bouquet. She looked back with bright smiling eyes and gently gave him a hug.

JANET

> (Whispered)
> Thank you.

He then took a small coil of rope from his belt and wrapped one end around her waist, tying it securely and the other tied to the center of the chains on her feet, lifting them up off the ground. Her hand resting on his shoulder he looked up at her and said…

GUARD

                    I can't remove them, but this will help.

This was another act of kindness, she was overwhelmed and replied
with a big smile. He stood up and took her hand and they both walked
down a trail, with woods on one side and the other side was thick
with straw grass. It emptied out on a long stretch of white beach,
which they had all to themselves. The waves were crashing on the
shore in a long hypnotic stretch. He took off his clothes and walked
into the water. Janet stepped in behind him and noticed it was as
warm as bath water.

He went under and then rose back up. Janet was reminded that he
needed the water to stay cool. As he was washing himself, she walked
up behind him and started to help. He took her hand and they walked
back to shallower water and he lay down with his back to a dune,
revealing his joy to be with her. The wind was strong but not angry,
and it helped push the waves into them, enhancing their new love for
each other.

They did not speak this entire time, but simply enjoyed each other.
Janet's thinking was that he is probably here against his will too
like her. He dressed and they slowly walked back. The closer they
got the slower Janet walked, pulling his arm tighter to her side.

Once near the end of the trail, she slowly let go and gave him a smile.
He pulled her towards him for one last embrace, causing her chains
to clink together.
                           JANET
                    (Returning his hug)
             I forgot they were there, the rope really
             helps. I am grateful to have found
             someone so nice in such a place.

Then they both headed back to their places, Janet at her post and
he to his. The other guard was at the water drum cooling himself
down, for the heat of the day was coming. Only the gentle one looked
back at Janet and smiled, then they disappeared into the woods.

Cat brushed the sand off her belly and legs saying,

                           CAT
             You were gone a long time. Did you have
             fun?
                           JANET
             Yes, he is very romantic. We went to a
             long beautiful beach.

Janet set the flowers off to one side, out of Cat's sight, next to
her towel. She was accumulating treasures.

Cat looked off to the sea and in a jealous soft voice…

CAT

Last night you came so easily.

JANET

(Smiling)
Yeah, I do like sex and the drink helped.

Cat then looked off into the woods, then to the water where that same boat was docking.

CAT

I can't do that.

JANET

Do what… Enjoy sex?

CAT

(With frustration)
Yes, I have never come.

JANET

Never?

CAT

Something is wrong with me, I know, but as hard as I try, I just can't seem to enjoy it.

JANET

You do know we are mammals designed for reproduction, don't you? I think you should let yourself go and just enjoy life more. You can't stop what is going to happen. So why not enjoy it? But, it would help if you had someone more romantic. Maybe he treats you badly, because you treat him badly. Try to be nicer.

In the morning light, Janet was admiring her blue feet and hands, gently brushing the sand off, trying not to smile so much. Cat looked over at her and said…

CAT

(Showing Janet her hands)
It comes off with time. It is some sort of paint.

JANET

No, I think it is some type of dye. Besides I like it.

CAT

(Sneered)
You look like a clown, hell we both do!

                         JANET
              (Smiling with a glare in her eye)
           You're very vain aren't you? Maybe that
           is why you can't enjoy life. You're too
           worried about how you look.

Cat then turned and moved to the back and threw up. She buried it
with the sand. Janet checked her pulse and temperature…

                         JANET
           I definitely think you're right, you're
           pregnant.

The back door of the pyramid lifted open. There seemed to be a lot
of activity going on. Voices were raised, not in anger but
excitement. Janet could hear the words…

                        A VOICE
              Finally, it starts.

Cat looked to Janet…
                          CAT
              What starts?

The guards were called in. They returned in about ten minutes with
two bowls for Cat and Janet. They said nothing to them, but Janet
could see something was up in her friend's eyes.

A short time later the girls appeared carrying suitcases. They took
them out to the dock by the boat. Next, a tall well dressed man with
dark hair appeared and the girls, who were also well dressed, joined
him in the boat as the skipper started the engine and they took off.

END SCENE

EXT.   MANUFACTURING COMPANY IN MEXICO – DAY

At the largest manufacturer of pseudoephedrine (mostly used for a drug called meth) for the pharmaceutical industry, a black car pulled up the drive, followed by two large box trucks. Lord now using the persona Jule with Tup-Con and Lee-Yaa at his side, doing their best to be dark-haired beautiful distractions, stepped out of the car.

Jule walked in carrying a briefcase and met with the sales agent. He opened his case and they verified that all his paperwork was in order. Jule had set up a scam pretending to be an executive from a large well known U.S. corporation, here to seal the deal. He had hacked into the corporation's banking system and showed a wire transfer paying for the drugs. The sales agent gave him a receipt. Jule then stepped back outside and pointed for the trucks to pull around back, where they were loaded with pallets.

The trucks pulled out and headed off in a cloud of dust with Tup-Con and Lee-Yaa at the wheels. As the car waited, sitting in the parking lot Jule made a call…

JULE/LORD

Now!

He then removed the battery from the phone and the car slowly drove away, down the same dusty road.

END SCENE

EXT.   RUN DOWN BUILDING - HOURS LATER

The trucks were parked outside another old run down building between two small towns. The car pulled up and parked in front. Jule walked in the front door, looked around and saw no one. He then walked to the back and there were the girls helping each other unload the trucks. Tup-Con covered in sweat, saw that Jule was there and pointed with her eyes to the back door saying…

> **TUP-CON**
> He has called twice now. I told him you
> were in the back checking the order.

Jule returned the call on the phone sitting on a small wooden table…

> **JULE**
> Yes sir, I am just calling to confirm that
> we will be there on time for your shut down.
> We do appreciate you letting us try out our
> new system. Yes sir, there is no charge.

After some pleasantries Jule wrapped up the call and joined the girls.

> **JULE**
> It's all going like clockwork.

The small crew now moved to transfer the drug called, pseudoephedrine - methamphetamine into large canvas bags. After they were sealed they covered them in a steel woven mesh fabric, then canvas again. The girls had removed their trucks' names and replaced the ad signs with new ones.

They both ran to help Jule load the bags into the newly designed plastic covers and sealed them closed. Then there were several small holes on each side that were used for the pumping of styrene, to prevent the bundles from sliding around.

They had created a new company that supplied newly designed cleaning plugs to scrape off the buildup of sludge on the oil company's pipeline from Mexico to the United States.

Tup-Con, Lee-Yaa and our Lord/Jule, walked out back and looked off into the distance. They kept checking their watches. Lee-Yaa looked up at him and said…

> **LEE-YAA**
> It should have happened by now.

Then suddenly off in the distance a cloud of black smoke rose and they heard a distant sound like thunder.

JULE

There.

The newly packaged plugs were loaded in. There was just enough time
left to clean and change for the next step. The two girls took some
time to stand there looking at the black smoke.

JULE

(Turning)
It begins, with the end of that poison; the
return of our land begins.

Jule walked away. He got back in his car and headed down the same
road with the girls in tow.

INT. OIL PUMPING STATION – NEXT DAY

At an oil pumping station south of the American border. The girls
were dressed to kill as they parked the trucks at the docks and then
met Jule at the door, where they walked him in. All are introduced.

JULE

(With a salesman's pitch)
We thank you for letting us try our new
graduated system for cleaning. This is
our first test and I am sure you will be
pleased.

They stepped to the back and watched the crew load the bags into the
oil pipeline that feeds from Mexico to the U.S.

JULE

(Turning to Tup-Con)
Is the other crew there to retrieve the
cleaning plugs?

TUP-CON

Oh yes sir, I received the confirmation
that they are there. I know you're going
to want them back to check for damage.

JULE

That's right. We want to see how well this
new system holds up.

As they stood there watching the last of the bundles being placed
in the pipe, they walked over to a tracking station so they could
see the movement of the cleaners as they move through the pipe. Jule
pointed to a panel on the wall showing every oil line and said…

JULE

Each plug has a tracking beacon attached
so we can ensure they all get through.
There, see they have now reached the U.S.

Jule turned to the manager with a smile…

JULE

Good, I know this is going to work and I
want to get there and see how they held up.
You should see a vast improvement in volume
now.

The manager checked the board as his eyes scanned over the gauges…

MANAGER

Good, that is what we all hoped for.

Jule then passed the manager an envelope filled with cash.

JULE

(Whispered)
This finishes our agreement.

Jule and the girls started moving to the door…

JULE

Is there a quicker way to the other side?

MANAGER

You can take our service road that follows
the pipeline. It would be quicker than
going through the border check point.

JULE

I was hoping we could do that and save the
time.

They traveled down a straight, paved road that turned and followed
the pipe. Soon they could see the U.S. border fence as they drove
north. The sun was setting so cooler air would help with the work
they have ahead of them.

The plugs were waiting for them in a pile; there was help to load
them in the back of the trucks. On the way back to Mexico, they
stopped by a locked gate that was still within the U.S. and turned
off their lights. It was very dark in the desert as they cut the
lock, swung open the gates, and took a detour, locking the gate behind
them.

INT.   CALIFORNIA MANUFACTURING PLANT – HOURS LATER

In the dead of night, they pulled up to an old manufacturing building and in through the large rusted open doorway. Once there, they waited in the dark. They got some badly needed sleep.

In the dawn's light, two cars pulled up. The exchange was about to be made. The girls stood at both sides of Jule, wide eyed, looking for trouble. A gang leader smiled as he held onto the two cases of money.

GANG LEADER

> What is to stop me from just killing you
> and taking the shipment?

Jule stepped in closer and looked at the man with a glare…

JULE

> First of all your boss would not like that,
> for you would not get any more shipments.
> Secondly, do you see that little red dot
> on your hand?

The gang leader looked down and saw the small red dot move up his arm and finally come to rest at his temple. They all quietly watched another dot appear from another angle on the same hand.

JULE

> Do you think I am that big of a fool to trust
> you?

Jule counted the money as Tup-Con and Lee-Yaa took their guns. As they backed the gang leader and his crew into a corner, the two sharp shooters climbed out of their points of seclusion and joined them at the door. Tup-Con brought the car up and they all climbed in. The marksmen were Miguel and Peppy. As they drove away with the cash, the gang members' guns were tossed on the driveway, just outside the building. Jule turned to speak to them all…

JULE

> You did a fine job and this will go a long
> way to fund the next projects that are
> unfolding, right now, as I speak.

The next day it was reported that the pseudoephedrine – methamphetamine plant burned to the ground. There were no deaths other than the owners of the plant. The equipment that makes the drug was destroyed beyond repair. A weapon from war was used to incinerate and melt the heart of the mechanism.

END SCENE

EXT.   LEAN-TO - DAY

Janet and Cat spent the morning talking as midday approached. Cat had been running on about her lost life and Janet grew tired of her whining once more. It was clear Cat was pregnant by just looking at her.

> **JANET**
> Is the feeling returning in your feet?

Cat picked out the last of the vines from her shackles.

> **CAT**
> (As she wiggled and pointed her toes)
> Yes, I have never felt such pain as what those two did to me. I can move them again, the feeling has returned.

> **JANET**
> They all seem to enjoy inflicting pain on you, why do you fight them so?

There was no response from Cat. Then Janet spotted her guard in the edge of the woods at the water can. He lifted the lid and took a scoop of water and poured it over his head. The other guard joined him for a drink and a cool down. Cat shifted in the sand to pull her legs out of the approaching afternoon sun. One of them stood off in the shade just looking at them, as the other started to walk over to Janet. Cat yelled at the standing guard…

> **CAT**
> You know we have no water over here!

He set the lid back in place while the nice one stopped and stood over Janet. After a moment he slowly reached in his belt and removed his canteen and handed it to her.

Still sitting on her knees, she remained motionless staring up at him with her blue eyes. Her blond hair blew gently in the soft breeze; she returned his kindness with a smile. He returned the same kind smile she saw last night and as she reached up to take his canteen their hands touched, giving both a spark of sexual excitement.

> **JANET**   V.O.
> He really is shy!

The sound of the water can lid broke the moment. Janet looked over to see the other guard pouring more water over himself. Cusi and Urpi appear from the woods to join the others.

He put the lid down and walked over as Cat pulled back and pressed up against her post, pulling in her legs. He saw Janet drinking from the other guard's canteen and removed his to give it to Cat; she reluctantly took it and had a long drink of water.

Janet almost emptied hers, but she shared a small drink with Cusi and Urpi, then put the lid back in place and looked over at the other guard.

                         JANET
          You do know she is pregnant with your
          child! Is this how you treat your women?
          Is this how you treat a gift from the Gods?
          Look at what you have done to her and how
          you treat her.

He widened his eyes in surprise at the news, but said nothing. Janet rose to her feet next to the other guard…

                         JANET
          We need food and Cat needs to walk down to
          the sea and wash off the dirt. She needs
          to soak in the salt water. It will help
          to heal her wounds.

Janet looked at both of them and heard the rumble of an empty stomach.

                         JANET
          You two have not eaten either, have you?

She moved closer and between them…

                         JANET
          Well can you two fish?
          (Turning to look at her guard with a smile)
          Thank you. By the way, I have a name.
          It's Janet. What is yours?

She handed him back an empty canteen.

                         MANI
          Mani, it means peanut. They named me
          that, because I was so small when I was
          born.
                         JANET
          Well good, then I will call you Mo.

She then looked over at the other guard…

                         JANET
          The mother of your child also has a name
          and it is Catena, she lets me call her Cat.
          I don't know what she will let you call her.
          Do you have a name?

He looked down at Cat with shame on his face, as Mo spoke for him…

                         MANI/MO
          His name is Tivu and I know he did not know
          she was with child.

Turning to Tivu, Janet said…
                          JANET
          Nice to meet you Tivu, I will call you Ter.
          Well she is and it's yours. Look at how
          you've treated her!

His face and shoulders showed Janet she had made her point.

                          JANET
          Please get me some soap and another towel
          for her.

Mo complied and Janet stood and watched Tivu, looking down at Cat
as she finished her drink and handed back the canteen. He moved
closer to Cat and gently removed the lock holding her collar, then
in the same manner removed the collar as well, revealing her raw
flesh. Cat looked over at Janet with wide eyes as she tried to get
up, but she was stiff and in pain. Ter helped her to her feet and
then slowly let go of her. Janet looked harshly at Cat.

                          JANET
          That was nice of Ter! What do you say when
          someone does something nice for you?

Cat, still looking surprised, turned to the sea and slowly started
to walk down the incline to the water, then turned back to Ter and
said…
                           CAT
          Thank you.

Janet noticed for the first time that Ter had the same skin as Mo
and the same affliction. Mo took her hand and they followed as Janet
rubbed his arm gently with her finger tips.

                          JANET   V.O.
          How would his skin breathe? How would the
          body expel fluids like salt?

Her mind was now concerned over his well-being.
As Cat waded into the warm sea water, Janet could tell that it felt
good to her.
                           MO
          There is no soap and towels for her.

JANET
Its okay, just the water will do wonders
for her.

Ter returned with a spear and was scanning the water for fresh food.
Mo started to build a small fire and in no time they had lunch going.

Janet noticed that Cusi and Urpi seemed to be staying back and just
watching as though waiting for a signal from someone. She spotted
a dish over by the drum by the woods where the guards cool themselves.
She went over to check to see if they had water and there was none.
Opening a small water spigot she cleaned the water dish and filled
it. The two dogs were staying back and looking around, until Jan
called them over for a drink. They came running over and were
grateful someone cared. She started petting them and talking to
them.

JANET
And what are your names? You're both so
pretty.

They seemed to love the kind attention. It was then she noticed one
is a girl and pregnant and the other a boy.

JANET
Oh my, someone is going to have puppies.
It must be the water here.

They drank all the water and she had to fill it again.

JANET
Well I don't know your names, so I will call
you Prince and Princess.

Cat was soaking in the warm water when she let out a squeal and stood
up splashing water.

CAT
(Screaming as she ran for the safety of the dock)
They're eating me!

Janet and the others smiled, as Mo told her…

MO
Those are Garra rufa fish. They eat only
the dead skin. They will help with the
infection.

CAT
But it's creepy!

JANET
Just do it. You need to soak and it is the
best we can do to clean you without (more)

soap. Then we'll reapply the antibiotics.

While the guards were cooking, Janet and Cat were alone, both soaking in the water. Looking toward the guards, Cat leaned over to Janet and said…

> **CAT**
> You really are taking chances by pushing them.

> **JANET**
> (With a big grin)
> No, I am not pushing them, you are by fighting them. I am only following the orders of our Lord.

All clean and shiny they started to have their lunch of fresh cooked fish when Janet reminded them of the dogs, Prince and Princess.

> **MO**
> We only have fish for them to eat.

Janet took on the responsibility of cleaning the last bits and started feeding them. They ate and licked her hands at the same time to thank her.

After they all ate, a cool breeze from a passing afternoon storm was enjoyed as the sun retreated behind the clouds.

Janet spotted a sore on Mo.

> **JANET**
> Take off your shirt.

She really wanted a better look at his unusual skin. He complied and before long they were walking down the beach for privacy to the water's edge. Once more they enjoyed each other.

Janet found she was drawn deeper into her new life each day. Her old life seemed to be locked behind another of the doors she had made to conceal painful memories. Demons held at bay behind thin covers that, at times, could be easily removed revealing much pain and a lot of anger. She was wallowing in waves of love and affection from someone kind. All new for her, in her new life, as she was enjoying every moment, her past was moving further behind her with each joy.

END SCENE

INT. WAREHOUSE - NIGHT

In a warehouse somewhere in the world, Jule was speaking to his new crew. He had the money now to hire the best and he did. Private collections were the easiest to hit. He would tell his new crew all the same thing…

>   **JULE**
>   I just want all the gold, silver and all
>   Inca items returned to me, you may have the
>   rest.

Jule wanted them to believe 100% in his cause.

>   **JULE**
>   They came to our land and stole our gold,
>   stole our silver and robbed the graves of
>   our most sacred temples. They tossed the
>   remains of our Gods around like trash as
>   they invaded the graves and stole. Now it
>   is our turn. Kill them if you wish, for
>   their lives have the same value as ours
>   did, none.

All over the world gold, silver, gems, cash, and Aztec and Mayan artifacts were being stolen from stores, banks, manufacturers and, best of all, museums and churches.

Every heist was carefully planned to the smallest detail. The deals were struck and Jule would fund the costs of each heist. Their take was to be only metals and the Incan items. Each criminal organization was glad to give up Jules's treasures, because its weight made it hard to dispose of. Besides the art, gems were worth more on the black market.

Then along came the biggest heist of all, the museum, where the only pages of Mayan text still survived. That was to be the biggest heist of all. Jule was there himself to retrieve the paper with his own hands. As the other Mayan and Aztec art and treasure were being removed, Jule stood motionless, holding the only text to have survived the Spanish Christians' invasions, destructions and thefts.

Mesmerized, he studied the text until Tup-Con broke his concentration.

>   **TUP-CON**
>   Now! We have to leave now!

And out into the night they slipped away.

DISOLVE TO:

EXT.   THE LEAN-TO – DAY

Janet had been marking the days on a post with a sharp stone. The Lord had been gone for three weeks to the day when Mo approached them. Off in a distance they could hear heavy trucks moving toward them.

> **MO**
> We have to move you to another location.

Without argument Janet stood and helped Cat up as well.

> **JANET**
> Is it far?

> **MO**
> No just a short way. You know the pit.

Janet stopped dead in her tracks and stared with widened eyes. Grabbing his arm, she looked at Mo saying nothing, only showing fear in her eyes as they filled with tears.

> **MO**
> (Smiled reassuringly)
> No, it's not that. I was told to move you
> both there for a short time. Do not worry,
> his plans for you is not death. Do not
> think that.

> **JANET**
> You're right. He would have done it by now
> if that were the case.

As the trucks and equipment grew closer Janet and Cat were marched to the rope ladder going down to the old basement of a house that had long since been blown away by a storm. There in the bottom was Ter, sweeping a clean place where he had set up an old mattress they had found.

They helped Cat down the ladder then Ter climbed out and stood at the top waiting for Mo. Janet walked over to Mo and they gently embraced.

> **JANET**
> You're not going to leave us here are you?

> **MO**
> No, I promise, before the end of this day,
> I will be back to get you out of here and
> things will be better, I promise.

Ter tapped on the wall with a stone as Mo looked up and turned to the ladder. Janet grabbed his arm…

JANET
Why does he not speak?

MO
He can't, he has never spoken.

Mo then climbed to the top taking the ladder with him. He looked back at Jan…

MO
It's only for a short time, I promise.

Then he smiled and walked away, as she listened to his footsteps walking away in the brush, hanging on every sound.

Leaning on the wall, Janet stared at the peeling paint as memories of her last time there came pouring back into her mind. An old door was opening and like a cold wind and the pain returned. She slowly turned to the images of a flooded basement with that gator hunting them. His cries of pain echoed off the walls as though he were there now. Janet looked over to where he last laid and then present day returned. The water was gone as well as Burt and the gator. Those memories slipped back behind the door.

When she returned to present day there in the pit, they first had silence as their companion. Then, they could only hear what sounded like heavy machinery moving the earth. The ground trembled at times, paint chips falling off the walls and Cat began to cry, as small chucks of the walls started to crumble.

CAT
They're never going to let us go!

JANET
You're right about that, but we can live
to escape, only if they trust us.

As Janet spoke, several more small parts of the walls fell to the floor and she began to look around. There in the corner of the pit something caught her eye. Sunlight reflected off a gold item just under the last remaining puddle of water. Janet walked over and there, next to the table leg with fresh gator marks she pulled up the broken chain with the gold cross that was once Burt's.

She held it close to her heart and looked up to the bright blue sky, closing her eyes, saying nothing as she clenched it. Like it was yesterday, she remembered the look in his eyes and began to yell at the sky…

JANET
You just used me as cover. You never ever
cared about what happened to me. Once a
cop, always a cop! When you said (more)

check it out, he meant for crime, not for
a nice place to go.

Looking to the blue sky she continued to yell…

> **JANET**
> Look what you did to me, you Christian
> bastard. I hope you rot in hell!

She stood there for a moment then she returned to the clean spot next to Cat and placed the gold necklace in the folds of her towel. Cat had stopped requiring comforting. She now feared Janet and her outburst. Janet was feeling her new power to speak up and defend herself as they waited.

Night was starting to fall and the bugs were starting to return as the noises above subsided and there was rustling in the leaves above. Suddenly, the rope ladder returned and both were helped out. Without saying a word they all walked the short distance back to the clearing where the pyramid was and as the sun was setting they stopped to see it was gone, completely gone. Not a trace of the towers, the pyramid, the hut or the dock. They were all gone, as though they were never there. Then she remembered Burt's words…

> **BURT**   V.O.
> *Would you like to go on a boat trip? No*
> *funny business, just a day on the water*
> *with lots of sun. There is a place I want*
> *to check.*

Janet turned to Mo taking his hand.

> **JANET**
> I want to see something, come with me.

Mo complied and they walked down to the sea and Janet stood staring off to the horizon. Then looking up to Mo she smiled…

> **JANET**
> I will miss this place. When are we moving
> out?

He smiled back at her…

> **MO**
> I too will take with me much fond memories,
> we move out tomorrow.

They both slowly turned in their own way saying goodbye to the sea as they headed back up the hill to their future.
Cat dropped to her knees and began sobbing; Janet knelt down and whispered in her ear…

> **JANET**
> Say nothing.

Then she looked up at Mo and Ter.

> **JANET**
> She is ok, it's just the baby.

Down by the beach Janet could see light coming from a small fire.

> **JANET**
> I hope that is dinner.

Ter walked over by Cat. Mo smiled at Jan…

> **MO**
> The breeze by the water will help keep the
> bugs away and we have food for you to eat.

Cat looked up at Ter and said…
> **CAT**
> Well, help me up.

So he did, without touching her, he walked by her side.

Cat looked at Ter and said…
> **CAT**
> Is it fish again?

Ter looked at her with a surprised look then smiled for the first time. Mo spoke for him…
> **MO**
> It's all the sea has to offer.

Cat smiled back…
> **CAT**
> I know.

After they ate, Janet and Mo slipped away and once more enjoyed each other in privacy as Prince and Princess stayed near. Afterwards, Janet tried to find out what plans they had for them.

> **JANET**
> Is it far away?

> **MO**
> Yes..

She lightly touched the skin on his chest, with her finger tips.

JANET

Will you be there?

MO

If he wants me to remain, I will. We all
owe him much.

Janet looked back at the fire where Cat was asleep with Ter standing
by her.

JANET

What will happen to us?

MO

I can't say for sure, but you are gifts from
the Gods. He must have a good place for
you all, a place of honor. He would not
bring dishonor to all of us by losing or
mistreating such gifts.

Janet turned back and looked at Mo, with surprise.

JANET

All… There are more than the two of us?

Mo saw the surprise in her eyes. He looked into her eyes and replied…

MO

Yes, there are four, counting you that I
know of.

Janet looked off into the dark where the sky blended with the sea.
Mo saw her pain and could do nothing to help.

MO

They are good people and you could do much
to help them with your gifts and with your
knowledge of how to help people. They are
not like the whites; they will appreciate
your help and show it.

Janet leaned over to rest her head on Mo's shoulder. Still saying
nothing, Mo stroked her hair and said…

MO

We should get some sleep; tomorrow will be
a long day.

DISOLVE TO:

EXT.   THE BEACH - MORNING

Janet woke to the sound of Mo's voice, but was unsure of what he said. She slowly sat up, but the sounds of the water lapping on the shore was hypnotic and made her want to fall back to sleep.

Finally, in the dim morning light she remembered where she was. Slowly sitting up, she looked down at her chains and remembered who she was. The blue was starting to wear away and this saddened her, for it had become a shield from her past, a guard protecting her from her past-life, now over. She looked out to the sea as the morning fog started to burn off. Touching her shackles, she smiled.

> **JANET**
> They too protect me from my past; they hold
> me here safe from what once was.

She looked off at Mo and Ter and her smile grew larger.

> **JANET**
> This is all to help me, to take me away from
> all the evil… they are guiding me to a safe
> and better future.

Janet had learned to compartmentalize bad things in her life and she had learned well how to survive finding good where she could. Over a decade of therapy had helped her with her past and now was to help shape her future. Feelings never seemed to matter, always belonging to some obscure concept that was just out of Janet's reach… until now.

Off in the distance, Mo was trying to get everything moving. Jan could hear him repeating…

> **MO**
> Wake up, it's time to go.

Panic raced through Cat's heart as she looked out to sea and thought…

> **CAT**   V.O.
> *No one is coming for me. No one is going*
> *to save me from this. We are just going*
> *to disappear, never to be heard from again.*

Then Janet thought of the pit where Cat had talked of carving a note on the wall.

> **JANET**   V.O.
> *What are the odds of anyone ever finding*
> *that? Slim to none and it still does not*
> *tell them where we are going. She is such*
> *a crybaby fool… I am growing tired of her.*

As Cat lay in a ball crying, Mo looked over at Janet shaking his head. He left her and came over to Janet, and she smiled up at him.

JANET
I am going to miss this place.

Still trying to get some fix on where they were taking them, she asked…

JANET
Will there be beaches like this, where we are going?

MO
Yes, but the air is dryer and the temperatures are colder at night and hotter during the day.

Janet looked back to the sea thinking, *'that was no help.'* She was flipping back and forth in her mind from looking forward to leaving her past and wanting help…

JANET   V.O.
At least here I had hope of someone finding me or us. But that ends today. What new hell lies before me? At least I knew this one.

She fought back her tears as she remembered her mother's cruelty and the early life she had in the dark basement.

She turned back to see that Mo had extended his hand to help her up and she took it. Holding onto her towel roll, rising to her feet, she looked down the beach to see Cat and Ter standing quietly. Cat wiped away tears as Ter stood and tried in his way to comfort her. Cat and Janet's eyes met for a moment, but they said nothing. As Janet stood brushing the sand from her towel, they began to follow their keepers up the cleared sand dune to the top, as the sun burst through the sea of fog.

As they walked for the trail heading into the woods, Cat started to tremble and let out a small squeal as she stopped dead in her tracks, then Cat took several steps back and fell down in the sand, curling up into a ball and uncontrollably sobbing and crying.

CAT
You're going to kill us!

Janet tried to comfort her and looked up at Mo…

JANET
Well are you?

Mo came and knelt next to her, trying to do his best to put her at ease…

                              MO
          No, that is not the plan. If anything
          happened to the two of you, we would
          probably be killed. You both are very
          special. I promise you, things are going
          to get better, soon.

Janet also spoke softly to Cat…

                            JANET
          If they were going to kill us they could
          have done it long ago. We have to trust
          them and do what they ask, so get up on your
          feet and walk.

Cat used every ounce of her courage to stand and face the future.
Her body was rigid as she walked partly bent over holding onto Janet.

                             CAT
          You'll stay with me, won't you? I am so
          scared.
                            JANET
          All we can do is trust them and hope things
          will get better. So hang on.

After a short walk they came to the pond where the burning water was
at one time, then to the old pavement appearing and disappearing under
their feet, their chains scraping smoothly across the cracked
decaying road. As they approached the old bridge they could see
beyond to the other side of the fallen tree, where a large truck was
parked. Cat bent down and picked up her chain so it would not get
caught on the jagged wooden planks. They slowly walked over the
broken boards to the other side and past the fallen tree to the truck.
Mo opened a door on the side revealing their future cell. Janet
looked closely at the sides, running her fingers over the blistering
dark red paint.
                            JANET
          This is a shipping container, isn't it?
          And the door is covered with thick
          Styrofoam for sound proofing so people
          can't hear our cries for help.

Janet quickly realized, by the look on Mo's face, that she should
not have said that.
                              MO
          The insulation is to keep out the heat and
          cold and to soften any blows if you should
          fall. There is food and water and even a
          small generator for the air-conditioning.

Janet touched Mo's arm and sheepishly smiled as Mo continued.

> **MO**
>
> And there are skylights as well as batteries for lights.

> **JANET**
>
> (Squeezing Mo's arm)
> I am sorry for what I said, will you help me up?

Mo climbed up inside to show where to step and extended his hand to Janet and she entered her new temporary home for the first time. As she looked around, it was just what he said. It was as nice and as clean as it could be. There were even two beds with bedding and a small rest room.

> **JANET**
>
> (Smiles)
> All the comforts of home.

Cat rubbed her belly and looked at Ter.

> **CAT**
>
> Well, are you going to help me or not!
> After all, it is your baby.

Ter softly smiled in his shy manner, he then quickly put down his gun and helped with both hands. Mo climbed down and turned to look back inside saying…

> **MO**
>
> I will check on you both as often as I can.
> When we are moving, try not to stand up for
> this will get bumpy from time to time.
> There is a shower, but try not to use much
> water, we must make it last.

Then they loaded Prince and Princess.

> **JANET**
>
> Be careful with Princess she too is pregnant.

Both men stopped for a moment then continued.

With the last of the cargo loaded, Mo looked in with a big smile.

> **MO**
>
> You all have plenty of food and water now.
> I will check on you. I promise it won't
> be too bad.

Then he reached over and slowly closed the door leaving them to their fate as he closed the heavy door and locked it in place.

Janet and Cat picked a bed and then Cat began to cry, curling up in a small ball. This time Janet couldn't hold it in and joined her. Prince and Princess joined Janet and tried to comfort her. She stopped feeling sorry for herself as she stroked them both with unconscious love. With practically no sounds from outside, their cell started to move. Shadows blocked the light coming from the skylight as they passed under trees. As Janet got control of herself she looked around to see marks on the walls showing signs they were not the first. She said nothing.

END SCENE

INT.   SHIPPING CONTAINER – EVENING

There was no way to keep track of time, but Janet tried to remember the turns made by the light's movement on the floor and walls, so she could build a map in her head. Somehow it helped to pass the time. Mo was true to his word and did open the door to check on the four of them several times. Cat turned away each time, but Janet's eyes lit up. Her thinking was turning this whole experience into being quite an adventure, as she started to look forward to each event with less fear. Their movement slowed and stopped several times and then there was nothing. Cat was still not taking this well and yelled out…

> CAT
> What is going on out there?

> JANET
> They're probably preparing to load us onto
> a ship. I hear heavy equipment out there.

> CAT
> A ship… Oh my god!

> JANET
> Yes, what did you think I meant when I said
> a shipping container? We are in for a long
> ride, Honey, and I am growing tired of your
> spoiled, self-centered, selfishness.
> Get over it!

Loud clunking sounds vibrated through the walls as the truck's clamps released the container from the truck. That did not help the emotional ride Cat was on. Then, from above, the sound of heavy clamps grabbing their cell pressing them to the floor as it pulled up quickly, both let out a scream.

It made several turns and twists rocking from side to side and finally stopped and settled down, then being clamped in place. They were in for a long ride indeed and it was now really sinking in for both of them. It was then that Janet noticed the air conditioning had been on all the time.

> JANET
> Let's just try to make the best of this.

She found the food and water just as Mo had said. Her nurse's training was kicking in…

> JANET
> Come on Cat, you're eating for two now.

> CAT
> (Hitting her stomach and screaming)
> I don't want this RAPE baby!

JANET

Don't do that again!!! It's not the
baby's fault and I hope you change your
mind. Just remember someone will want the
child if you don't.

CAT

(Yelling)
Then they can carry it!

They finally fell asleep.

Suddenly, the cell door opened and fresh heavy sea air raced in as
the winds whipped past. Sounds from the outside poured in as well
as smells of heat from the day. It was Mo's voice coming from the
dim light…

MO

Are you all ok?

CAT

(Snapped)
You did not kill us yet!

JANET

We are fine and thanks' for checking on us.

Mo stepped in and stood in the doorway…

MO

You can come to the door to get some fresh
air and have a look. It's a nice view.

By now Prince and Princess had joined Mo, so Janet took him up on
the offer as well, for she wanted to add the location to her map in
her head. She slowly walked over and Mo stepped out in front of her
on to the top of another container and looked around with her.

MO

(Pointing)
That is the front of the ship. We had them
place us here on the top near the edge with
one container as a deck overlooking the
side.

As Janet moves closer to the doorway she could see they were still
in port, slowly moving out to sea. She tried to make out the sky
line of a city to help understand where they were. It was filled
with sky scrapers. Mo stood firmly on the roof of the container just
before the edge, then came back to help Janet. She rested her arms
on Mo's shoulders as she leaned on him to get a better look, rising
on the balls of her feet.

JANET

I am surprised you would open the door, aren't you afraid someone will see us?

MO

(Laughs)
This ship moves thousands of people around the world every year, maybe every month. Slavery is a big business, coming into countries and going out. Mostly the sex trade, that is. If you have the money then you can buy anything… anyone.

Janet's arm went limp and slid down Mo's back as she returned her heels to the floor.

JANET

Is that the plan, selling us into slavery or the sex trade?

Mo turned and slowly gave her that same gentle smile.

MO

No, our Lord is not a pimp. If he were, you would be packed in here like sardines and we would not care for your comfort. He is a very special man and you will find this out. Do not fight him like that one.

Looking to the inside, pointing with his eyes.

MO

And there is one more thing, if all he wanted from you was money, I would gladly pay the price. You are much more valuable than money.

Mo and Janet move to the side to let Ter in and he joined Cat on the edge of the bed. She turned her back and pulled away to one side, as close to the wall as she could get, while he lay back and fell asleep. Mo sat down on the doorway, opened a pack of cigars and lit one, leaning back to enjoy the view.

JANET

May I join you?

Janet looked out the door further to see the view of the front of the ship. They were at least ten stories up and the smell of burning fuel sometimes drifted by in the strong wind, while they were moving.

Janet tried to step on the roof of the container next to them where Mo was resting his feet and she could feel the heat still in the container roof from the sun. She briefly recoiled, then braved the heat; it was not so bad after all. She could see down between the containers. It was a long drop down.

She shared her water with Mo and they sat there and watched the coastline disappear into the blackness thinking…

JANET

> *He is my only link to whatever is before me, I had better take care not to burn any bridges. Besides I could be stuck with one much worse. Indeed, I better take care of this one.*

V.O.

As darkness replaced their view of endless white caps, lights from the ship made an eerie glow on the passing fog. The cooling night air helped to cool down the roof and so, Janet moved closer to Mo holding his arm and feeling chilled.

JANET

Do you want something to eat?

MO

No, I am done for the day.

As he flicked his smoke out to the sea, they retreated to their bed where Mo stood looking down at her, Prince, and Princess.

MO
(Smiled)

What about me?

Janet looked up and returned his smile as she pats a small place to her side. Mo sat down and let out a short sigh. He then removed his clothes. They both took a quick shower and once more they enjoy each other in the dark.

When morning came Janet found she was alone in bed and looked over to Cat sitting on the edge of her bed softly crying. She is tired of trying to comfort Cat, so as she sat up she said…

JANET

You have to adjust to this. You are here…
so make the best of it. For heaven sakes
we are not in that pit. There are no bugs
eating us alive and we're not chained to
a pole.

Cat pointed down and Janet sees that Cat is chained to the floor. Janet checked to see if she was also chained, but she was not and said…

JANET
What has happened now, Cat?

CAT
(Pointing to the lock)
I told him the first chance I got I was going to jump, so he did this.

JANET
That was stupid. I told you to keep your mouth shut. Haven't you gone through enough pain yet? You keep fighting them. Don't you get it? They're always going to win. Make the best of it, stop fighting them.

There was a sound outside as Mo opened the door and looked in, carrying breakfast. The smile fell off his face as he looked at Cat then at Janet.

MO
She said she was going to jump.

Janet glared at Cat and then looked at Mo. Mo turned to Janet…

MO
Are *you* going to jump?

JANET
No, I am harder to get rid of then that.

MO
(Smiled)
Well, suit yourself, Cat.

He moved to join Janet on the bed with food for all, including Prince and Princess. As Janet gained more and more of Mo's trust, they would leave her alone. A week into the voyage she noticed one of the walls was made of boxes. She pulled one down and carefully opened it to discover it was full of C.D.s. As she pulled one out and read the cover, it meant nothing until she looked closer. It read:

Death by Being Eaten Alive
Produced by Blood, Guts and Mayhem productions

There was a grainy photo of the pit and it was her and Burt facing the gator. There were more photos on the back and offers of watching a man being eaten alive.

She slowly returned the C.D. to its proper place in silent memory of that time, and his screams filled her head until the lid was sealed tightly. Streams of tears ran down her face as she returned the box and sat back down on her bed. As she grabbed her towel to wipe her eyes, part of the gold chain brushed her fingers. She tucked it back in, saying nothing while hiding her memories. She closed that door in her mind and the tears stopped.

> **JANET**
> (Whispers)
> You are stronger now, you can cry. Feelings are a growing part of who this new Janet is becoming.

DISOLVE TO:

EXT.   PANAMA CANAL – DAYS LATER

Janet awoke to find both men talking outside.

> **MO**
> Oh good… You're awake. Come see Janet.

The air was full of the sounds of seagulls and the horizon was full of trees.

> **MO**
> It's the Panama Canal!

As Janet gently placed her hand on his neck, she took in the sights of all the trees, birds and the locks. She turned to Cat…

> **JANET**
> It's so beautiful. Would you like to see?

There was no response.

> **JANET**
> I am sure they would let you come to the doorway to look.

Cat simply rolled over in bed to face the wall saying nothing. Turning back to Mo and Ter, Janet said…

> **JANET**
> I grow tired of her.

Janet had lost track of time as each day passed, traveling through this land. They both had lots of time to spend together and would drag the mattress out to the deck and lean part of it against the wall for comfort. Each day, they were joined by Prince and Princess, whose pregnancy is now starting to really show.

> **JANET**
> It is like a slow moving post card. (more)

I want to try to remember each turn of the
canal, each hill and all the wild life.

                    MO
             (Points)
The trees are all gone, I can't remember
the last time I saw the old man of the
forest.   He is called the Orangutan.
They may have killed them all by now.   They
have destroyed this land.

Janet looked over at Mo and saw the look on his face.   It showed that
he was saddened by what he saw.

                  JANET
             (Comfortingly)
Not all are dead; there are still the ones
in the zoos.   If that is any help.   We know
those won't be eaten.

Mo smiled back and took Janet's hand.   She leaned over and rested
her head on his shoulder, looking at their entwined hands…

                  JANET
             (Smiled)
This is like a vacation.

                  JANET   V.O.
I am really starting to fall for the guy.
I had better enjoy this time for I do not
know what is to come.

Janet feared she would alienate Mo if she asked anymore questions,
so she was content to just wait for him to talk about it.   Once at
the end of the canal, the big ship picked up speed, turned and headed
south.

DISOLVE TO:

EXT.   SHIP'S PORT - DAY

Several days later they finally arrived in another port.   The horizon
showed fewer and fewer cities along their path, but this was such
a big port.
                  JANET
             (Turned to Mo)
Why is there such a big port here?   There
seems to be no people to justify one.

MO smiled and pointed to a new road full of trucks with shipping
containers…

MO

See… over there are the largest soybean plantations in the world. It is a place I once visited with my father and played as a child. Everything is made out of soybeans today. Like I said, they have cut down all the trees to grow beans.

Janet saw sadness on Mo's face…

JANET

All for money! What about the land, the plants and the animals that once lived here?

MO

I guess they're all dead. That very fact, really angers our Lord. He is doing his best to stop them and save what land and life he can.

DISOLVE TO:

INT. SHIPPING CONTAINER – DAY

The ship docked. Once more the door was closed and Mo and Ter left them. Soon the cell was lifted and then fastened to another truck.

For Janet, the longest moments of the trip moved by, for she felt she could never be rescued now. All hope was gone as she tried to keep track of her map in her head. Cat was curled up in a ball once more sobbing as Janet started to really worry. She unconsciously pushed herself back into the Styrofoam wall pulling her legs in as though it would protect her from what lay beyond the door.

The road trip took three days. At the end of each day, Mo and Ter would open the door to let in fresh air, bring food and water and let the dogs out to run. When Janet could look, she saw only forest and rocks. The truck slowed to a crawl as branches scraped over the skylight. Miles of slow bumpy road with low branches meant it was a road less traveled. The truck slowed to a halt under a large tree.

It was a heart piercing emotional moment, hearing a metal snap at the door, when it opened and the light from this new life poured in, with a blinding view. There were no sounds at first, then the cry of a macaw and the sounds of keys.

Janet stared at the blinding light as she moved over to Cat as though it would help. But Cat's fear was now causing Janet to tremble as well. It was a long journey to get to this place and all manner of evil was coming out of Janet's mind, as those black doors from her past were opening.

Prince stood at the door guarding them as Princess waddled over by Janet to give her comfort, sensing her fear. Her licks of comfort brought Janet back to reality. Her eyes started to adjust to the light. She was now shaking uncontrollably, afraid of the unknown. Cool, dry, clean air started to replace the stale air from the long journey in their cell.

Mo was the first to look in and saw the tragedy unfolding before his eyes. He was greeted by Prince and as Mo petted him he just started talking in a reassuring voice. He signaled to the others behind him to back away and be silent as he tried to reassure his cargo all was fine. He stood there talking for a few minutes as his long time friends greeted him with licks of reassurance. Mo put a smile in his voice…

MO

> Come on you two, we have arrived home and
> there is much to see.

But he got no response other than trembles from fear. Prince and Princess were first out. A shadow crept along the floor. The silhouette of a man, with a familiar voice, Janet knew that it was Mo and he was talking…

MO

> You can come out now. Please calm down,
> this is a good place and you are safe here.
> I have much I want to show you. It is time
> for you to come out and see.

By now both Ter and Mo had climbed in and stood for a moment, looking at the fear. Mo knelt down with a smile to reassure Janet and it did as she slowly started coming back. Ter knelt down to remove the lock that held Cat's shackles to the floor and then stood back by the door. No one moved. Mo could see he needed to say more, so he pointed out the door…

MO

> There are all the things I spoke of here,
> just out that door and I know you are going
> to enjoy it with me. There is fresh food
> and water and there is also a place for you
> to shower over there. Your journey is
> over and you are home now. Well, my home
> and I hope you will like it and come to love
> it as I do.

Janet's trembling subsided as her blue eyes re-focused on a face she had grown to trust and love.

JANET

> You're not going to hurt me? Please don't
> hurt me.

Mo gently took her hand as tears filled his eyes…

                              MO
         I promise you, I will stand before any pain
         that comes at you.   I know in your past you
         have suffered unimaginable pain… I can see
         that… and I can't fix it… but I can help
         today.   I love you and I will protect you
         from harm.   Come and see this place and you
         too will fall in love with it.

Janet and Mo rose to their feet and embraced in silent peace as though
they were the only people in the world.   For them they were.   Still
Cat did not move.   She just looked at the wall away from Mo and Ter
in disbelief.   Mo, still trying to help, added…

                              MO
         The nights get cold here. So we also have
         warm clothes for both of you.

Mo then reached down and took Janet by the hand.

                              MO
         It's not a bad place.   The worst is over
         now.   Come and see with me.

                         WOMAN'S VOICE
         Well are you going to bring them out or
         what?

                     SECOND WOMAN'S VOICE
          Yeah, let's see what you brought us.

Janet slowly squeezed Mo's hand like a vice and turned to the doorway
and asked…
                            JANET
         Are you going to leave me?

                              MO
         I will never leave you, unless our Lord
         asks me to.   Otherwise you are stuck with
         me.

As she got closer to the doorway, she squinted her eyes in order to
see through the bright morning light.   The first woman yells up at
them…
                           WOMAN #1
         Well, well, well Mo.   You're right. You
         did get a pretty one.   Well, Honey, you're
         our first blonde.   One of you big lugs
         needs to get down here and help that poor
         girl down from there.

Janet could see a large woman with a big booming voice.

WOMAN #1
I can help. Look at me.

Mo jumped down and once more offered help to Janet as she looked out the door for the first time at her new surroundings. There was a collection of small, stone walled, buildings, making up a sort of residence. Each looked as though it was tossed there like a die from your hand and just landed where it did without plans.

Some of the one story buildings were using the cliff walls as part of their design. Others were up against the walls of other buildings and still others were carved into the wall of the cliffs like caves.

The sparse covered hills turned into mountains that seemed to go on forever as Janet's eyes followed the road's end to a smaller path. Looking down at those who were there to greet them, Janet smiled…

JANET
Wow, this really *is* the end of the road.

The booming voice belonged to an older bigger woman that smiled back and then snapped orders at the men…

WOMAN #1
(In a strong friendly voice)
Help her down Mo. Who else do you have in
there? Bring her out. What is going on
in there? Come out, Hon. Don't you want
to get out of there?
Janet was on the ground looking around with Princess at her side, sees Cat appear at the door. Janet warned them…

JANET
I am sure you can see she is pregnant, but
not like you.

Looking at the big woman, she said…

JANET
You must be due any day now. You should
not be on your feet.

WOMAN #1
That's sweet of you to notice, Hon, but if
we don't do it, it don't get done.

Concerned of the well being of the woman's child, Janet asked…

                         JANET
           Have you seen a doctor yet?

                        WOMAN #1
          (Holding her pregnant tummy and smiling)
          Look around you, Hon. We are it.

Mo had lifted Janet down to the muddy clay-like brown earth. The
cool mud squirted between her blue toes. She looked at the bright
green trees covered in vines that have created patches of dark green
shadows that mix in with a sprinkling of wild flowers. This is all
growing between large stones piled everywhere.

                          MO
                Let me show you where the shower is so you
                can get cleaned up. Then we'll get some
                food in you. After that, if you are up to
                it, we will go for a walk.

They both stood there looking back at the container.

                          MO
                But first, let me help get Cat out.

Janet grabbed Mo's hand and pulled at it.

                         JANET
                Leave her alone. She will come out when
                she wants.

Looking over to the woman Janet smiles…

                         JANET
                She has made this as hard as she can on
                herself, so let her stay in that box.

Turning to the big woman…
                         JANET
                By the way, I am called Janet.

The big woman smiles back…
                         PABA
                I am Paba… It means, mother. Welcome to
                your new home.

Behind one of the scattered small stone buildings was a community
shower. A large drum filled with water stood on four wooden legs
and Janet was shown how to open a valve to let the water down. Mo
and Ter were now filling the drum with stream water using buckets.
The sun had warmed the water that was there in the drum and the new
water was ice cold as it came from a stream deep in the mountains.

While she was showering, Mo retrieved Janet's towel from the cell and as he returned it to her he felt something in the roll. As he slowly unwound it, he wondered what she would have hidden. There, deep in the folds was a small sea shell. It reminded him of their times on the beach so far from this place. He held it to his nose and could still smell the sea. He gently rolled it back up and returned it to her, walking away to give her privacy.

She watched him set it down on a stone nearby. He said nothing. When she stepped out she checked it and found the shell and further down was the gold chain still hiding. It was time to find a better place to hide it. She looked around while she had her privacy and she found a safe place in the mud under one of the shower stones. She buried Burt's cross and chain there and rinsed her hands as she prepared to join the others, to dry herself in the warm sun. As she turned the corner she met Mo waiting his turn to shower.

JANET

(Smiles)
You could have joined me.

MO

I thought of it, but there are too many
people now, besides I had things to do.

He wrapped a rope around Janet's waist tying it tightly and the other end around the center of her chains.

MO

There, that is all I can do to help make
things better.

There on his knees Janet held his head near her. He rubbed her ankle and then the other, checking them for sores. He remained motionless for a moment…

MO

I am sorry… I wish I could do more.

Food was prepared while Mo took his turn to clean up. Janet stayed true to Prince and Princess, feeding them and making them a bed for the upcoming litter. When Mo joined them inside, the girls were all talking a mile a minute.

Mo stood in the small doorway. It was the first time Janet had seen him without his camouflage uniform… other than naked. He stood there wearing old blue jeans and a bright yellow T-shirt with no shoes on his feet. He joined them at the table, Ter and Mo tolerated the chatter, watched and ate their local foods. Mo could hardly keep his eyes off Janet, for she was now wearing a wool sweater and a long wool skirt provided by the locals that help to hide her chains.

INT.   STONE VILLIAGE - EVENING

After they ate, Mo could stand the chatter no more and took Janet
by the hand.

MO

Come with me, I want to show you something.

They both stood up and headed for the front door.

PABA

You had better take a blanket, because it
gets cold up there.

Mo turned, smiled and took a brightly colored, handmade blanket from
the pile of donations. Janet first checked on Princess and her
upcoming event, smiled and told them both…

JANET

I will be back. You two wait here for me,
ok?

Outside Janet saw the door to the cell wide open and knew Cat was
still inside. She went over and slammed the door shut and latched
it closed.

JANET

Let the poor little rich girl stay in there
and cry. She has food and water. Maybe
tomorrow she will want to join us.

Mo took Janet by the hand, and they headed to the end of the road
that turned into a dirt path rutted by the rain. For now it was just
dust and rocks under leaves and branches. The path took a sharp
incline and started to become treacherous, Janet did her best to keep
up.

A canopy of trees covered the steep earth as they came to steps carved
in the rock long ago. These steps were worn down by thousands of
feet walking this way, long before Janet. As she took her first step
on the stone steps, she could feel a connection with those people
before her.

MO

(Smiled)
I never wear shoes here out of respect for
those that built this. Shoes wear down
the stone faster. Besides I feel a closer
connection to those before me.

Mo had to tie the blanket around his slender waist, for they would
need both hands for the next climb. As Janet followed Mo, they neared
a cliff's edge that grew more and more precarious. It was a long
way down.

                         MO
          Don't worry, just step where I step and
          grab what I grab.

The trees turned into a forest filled with life. Mo seemed to spot
it all, pointing each out to Janet. Finally, there was blue sky
ahead, Janet was out of breath. So Mo slowed down and they began
to take breaks along the path, stopping to enjoy the spectacular
views.

                         MO
          Come on. It's only a short way to the top
          and then you will see something that I bet
          will take your breath away.

Janet whined as they continued to climb and finally reached the top.

                       JANET
          My breath is already taken away from this
          hike.

Mo sat on a flat stone and watched Janet's eyes and her facial
expressions when she looked upon the restoration site of Machu
Picchu.
                       JANET
          (Softly with reverence)
          It's amazing!

                         MO
          Come on. We will go there and I will show
          you more.
                       JANET
          Wait a minute. Isn't that a road over
          there?
                         MO
          Yes, for tourists, but they don't have this
          view. Come on, there is much to see.

Down the side of the cliff they follow the less traveled path as it
winds around the side of the cliff. They find themselves at the base
looking up at more stone stairs, worn down by the feet of hundreds
of thousands of people over countless years. Mo took Janet's hand
and smiled like never before. His eyes were filled with excitement
as he lifted his right foot slowly and placed it on the first step.

                         MO
          There is only one way to truly observe the
          whole of this Huala or sacred place. You
          must feel each stone, hand carved and laid
          here for us to walk on, and you can't take
          it all in wearing shoes. I always find I
          can connect with those of the past (more)

by fully touching what they have touched.
For me, they are still in the stone.

The sun was starting to slip behind the peaks. The stones in the sun were still warm, but the shadows revealed the cold that was to come.

> **JANET**
> I bet it gets cold here at night.

> **MO**
> We will be fine.

As they climbed the steps returning to the warmth of the sun, Mo would stop at each plateau pointing out to Janet with much joy…

> **MO**
> The rain water is caught and run through a series of stone terraces filled with the quarried chips made to hold the water. Then covered with earth for growing of food, like corn and it works still to this day.

At the top, are all of the stone buildings so artfully assembled that the lacing of squared stones, like all the Inca sites, they were a thing to be marveled at. A stream of water traveled through the center of the structures in a series of hand carved trenches and pipes. They both took a drink. Mo pressed on telling her about every structure.   It was then that Mo took Janet to the highest point, where an oddly carved stone shaped in a collection of squared blocks stood.

> **MO**
> This is a Huala, a very sacred place. We stand in the center of all life here.

He pointed to the four mountain tops surrounding them…

> **MO**
> This point is the center and below, surrounding us, is the river of life. This is where communication with the Gods would take place. I can feel the ground vibrate with the power that is here.

Mo looked to the sky, closing his eyes. Once more fear raced through Janet's body as she wondered if this was *her* fate. She backed away from the stone and she said…

> **JANET**
> This is where they sacrificed people. I can almost smell the blood.

Mo once more returned to earth and smiled at Janet reassuringly, as she tried to figure out her place in all of this. She often studied his face and his high cheek bones, but they were not as high as others she had seen. Clearly there was more than one line of Indian descendents, but that did not explain his skin. Mo saw the fear in her eyes and asked…

MO

> Did I frighten you with all of this?

JANET

> No, I enjoyed hearing the stories. You
> bring the place to life like a tour guide,
> only I don't understand you.

By now the sun was setting and the cool air was descending and Mo moved to embrace Janet.

MO

> I will tell you one day soon. There is
> much going on and each of us plays a part
> in a much bigger picture. There is much
> that I don't know myself, but I trust the
> Lord completely.

They smelled smoke coming from below and Janet saw that they were not alone. Several others were cooking at a small campfire. They joined two other couples down another set of stairs. Janet was the only one with white skin, yet she was welcomed with respect, as one of them. There was a small stone room with no windows and a cloth blanket covering the door.

Mo noticed that Janet was shivering, so he gave her the blanket he was carrying. The others brought them food and bowed respectfully to Janet, for they knew who she was and paid no attention to her chains.

They quickly ate and, like the others, found a place to bed down out of the wind. Hot embers along with hot stones from the fire helped to keep the room warm during the night. As they exchanged body heat, Janet could keep it in no more so she asked…

JANET

> What is going to happen to me?

Mo pulled back and she could see him smile at her by the dim fire light.

MO

> You are a gift. I don't have all the
> answers, but the Gods spoke of you and the
> others. That is why I am here as well as
> Ter; we were told of your coming and the
> power you would bring.

> **JANET**
>
> What… power?
>
> **MO**
>
> Yes. I was told the Gods spoke to Pachacuti and he told me what they said. That is why I am here with you.

Janet looked at the fire and turned back to Mo…

> **JANET**
>
> What did the Gods say?

Mo rubbed his legs and looked deep into the fire for a long moment, then said…

> **MO**
>
> He told me I was part of a nearly extinct people and that we are but a few that have survived the extermination by the Christians, hundreds of years ago.

Janet took his hand.

> **JANET**
>
> So that helps me understand some of his hatred of Christians, but I am to bring something. Will I end up on that block to take a message to these Gods in some sort of sacrifice?

Mo looked back at Janet with a surprised look turning to anger.

> **MO**
>
> Listen to me. You are a gift from the Gods. It would anger them to no end if we did such a thing and he knows this. You don't seem to understand. You are very special and what you bring is yet to be seen or explained to me or us. But the Gods know and I trust in them, and you should too.

Across the room, other couples were enjoying themselves, intertwined in love. It was an intoxicating sight and the whole of the day was spinning in her head as she found herself rubbing her ankles under the shared blanket. She and Mo, both still leaning against the stone wall, found themselves staring deeply into the small fire. Janet was rubbing the handmade stones with her toes, feeling the tight seams of the makers, leaned over to whisper…

> **JANET**
>
> How many babies do you think this place has made?

She looked at their fellow companions and smiled. Her eyes reflected the firelight as she slipped down to the floor. Mo slowly embraced her under the covers and they join the others in showing their love for each other.

DISOLVE TO:

EXT. MACHU PICCU – MORNING

The sun broke over the mountain tops as Janet woke. She could smell food. As she opened her eyes, Mo was returning with something for all of them, water. She sat up as the others were catering to them and watching for their reaction. She could see they had become the center of their attention. She smiled at those that prepared the food…

> **JANET**
> Oh this is very good, thank you.

Turning to MO she whispered…

> **JANET**
> They seem to hang on our every word. We must be quite a sight to them.

She thought of how strange a sight she must be to them; a blond with blue eyes and remnants of bright blue on her hands, feet, and face. Then there was Mo with his unique skin. She smiled at each smiling stare. Mo then took Janet outside and they warmed in the morning sun. Then he took her by the hand and he gave her a full tour of the entire fortress/palace.

> **MO**
> Over here is the palace of Pachacuti the King. He is a God, you know. When he was alive he brought all of us together and found this Huala… this sacred place. I was told he was a visionary and the only God to see this place. That is what brought people together. When he died he was mummified and still is cared for to this day by the Panaca, keepers of the dead King. Tup-Con and Lee-Yaa are the daughters of those families that care for him. They are entrusted with the well being of the body that houses the Lord King. They have trained all their lives to be the Panaca.
>
> Some of the other Kings were very bad, killing their people for the Gods. There were always sacrifices to the Gods, but he killed only the enemies of us all. The other ones would kill their own people. The Spanish came with two hundred (more)

> soldiers and no one stopped them. Most
> all hated the other Kings so much they let
> the country fall to the Spanish. Only
> they brought slavery and disease that
> destroyed the country. The Christian
> Spanish killed off 95% of the people in
> some cities. The Christians enslaved the
> people for over 300 years, stealing all the
> gold and silver they could.

Janet tried to say nothing; she could see he was feeling every ounce of their pain. She had learned to let a teacher teach and not to ask questions until you are asked.

                    MO
> I have lived here all my life and when I
> was a young boy, I heard of a child that
> was the reincarnation of Pachacuti. He
> was very small and knew of things no one
> could have known. He held secrets that
> only the Panaca knew and they tested him
> for days until he grew tired of it and
> started telling them all what to do. He
> was to be the new God King.

Mo stopped talking and started to pull back. Disappointment filled his eyes.

                    MO
> I am boring you. You don't want to hear
> all of this.

Janet grabbed his arm…

                    JANET
> No, no, you're wrong, I want to hear more.
> I just did not want to interrupt you while
> you were talking.

She smiled at Mo and he returned the smile.

                    JANET
> So tell me how did you meet him? Where and
> what was it like?

                    MO
> He was being taken from city to city, per
> his request and he pointed to me in the
> crowd and yelled out the name Maita. I was
> pushed to the front and he started telling
> me of his plans. I never questioned him,
> he knew so much and he wanted to restore
> his people to the once greatness (more)

they had enjoyed.   But the land was
stripped clean by the invading Spanish
Christians; and they had taken our Gods
away, he told me.   They replaced them with
their foreign God so they could control us.

Mo and Janet had walked most of the grounds and enjoyed the views
of each of the four God Mountains, and the sacred river that flowed
below.   Janet lightly touching her finger to the seam in one of the
walls and spoke softly…

                    JANET
          So how did he know your name?

                     MO
          That is not my name, remember I am Mani,
          but I found out later 'Maita' was a good
          Priest he knew in his other life.   I have
          no memory of such a life, nor did I ever.
          But he was so sure and believed me to be
          this person that I could not and would not
          bring shame upon my family by questioning
          him.   Whatever he asked of me, I will do.
          He knows what I don't and sees what I
          cannot.

Janet was having stronger feelings for Mo and wondered if it was what
Patty Hearst went through when she was kidnapped; or were they real
feelings of deep love.   She thought of her life before and now.
Janet wondered as she looked out over the sparkling water in the river
below.

                    JANET
          What does he; this Lord see for me? How do
          I fit into all this?

Mo moved in slowly and put his arms around her.

                     MO
          All I know, I will tell you.   He told us
          all there will be gifts from the Gods as
          a sign of their return and to show all he
          is on the right path.   You and the others
          are the gifts in his vision. Gifts from
          the gods, you all are very special people.
          I don't think I was much over ten at the
          time when he spoke of you.   He said, 'A
          woman will come into your life.   She is
          most special.   Treat her so, for she comes
          from the Ayar or Family of Sun God and you
          will be able to tell.'

Mo then released his gentle hold on Janet and took one step back, looking deeply in to her eyes.

                              MO

                    I have looked for you all my life and I have
                    a heart full of love for you.   If I
                    displease you, please tell me and I will
                    stay away. I want you to know, I did as
                    I was told, as I am now. You are most
                    special and I wish only to treat you so.
                    If I have failed, please tell me.

His hands were trembling at the thought of her rejecting him. Janet
slowly stepped closer and looked deeply into his eyes, without saying
a word.   Tears were streaming down her face as she moved to him slowly
and put his arms around her back whispering…

                            JANET

                    I love you.

She embraced him gently and silently. They stood there for a moment.
She felt a sense of euphoria and tingling in her body.

                            JANET

                    Am I starting to glow?

                              MO

                    Yes, you are blinding me.

They continued standing there soaking up the moment in the sunlight,
as Janet thought… *I have a lot of power, if I use it right.*

                            JANET

                    Do you have another woman, or would you
                    prefer one of the others?

Mo tightens his hold on her.

                              MO

                    I have never been with a woman before you…
                    you know that. I was told you were coming
                    and I could think of no one else.

                            JANET

                    Looks like both of us are in this by design.
                    If I have your child, will you care for us
                    or is your job done then?

                              MO

                    There is no 'job done.' I do what my Lord
                    asks of me and will remain at your side if
                    this is what he wants. But if I displease
                    you, he need not know we are not intimate.

Janet buried her face deep into Mo's chest and said…

> **JANET**
> I sometimes ask harsh questions or say cold
> things. It is because I was not given what
> you have, and I had to learn how to express
> myself. I am still discovering feelings
> that most have used all their lives. If
> I am cold, harsh or distant, you must tell
> me and show me, for it is not in me, but
> know I am trying.

Janet returned the strong embrace, thinking, '*I am so turned on by this man and all of this.*' She pushes back away from Mo and he had a disappointed look come over his face. She smiled at him and took his hand and pulled him into one of the small rooms where she showed him how she felt. They reemerge from the magic of the moment full of smiles for each other, as Mo looks to the sky saying…

> **MO**
> It's getting late. We should start
> heading back before the tour buses start
> to come.
> **JANET**
> Thank you for bringing me here and sharing
> your life with me.

They headed back down the trail that wanders back through the trees overlooking Machu Picchu, and then Janet stopped Mo.

> **JANET**
> (Pointing)
> There is a road down there why don't we see
> more people?
> **MO**
> They will come by midday. Our Lords first
> plan was to tell them that the bridge was
> out, to stop the tourists. He plans to
> reclaim his place and he let them clean it
> for him.

They returned to their new home and Janet started to check on all the other inhabitants including Cat who was sitting by the fire looking away. Before the sun set, Janet returned to the shower and retrieved the gold chain and image of the Christian God. In front of everyone she placed it in Mo's hand.

> **JANET**
> Give this to our Lord and ask him why he
> treats his gifts as slaves, in chains.

The room went still and quiet. Only the sound of the fire could be heard as Mo's stunned face turned soft, in the last rays of sunlight.

                    MO
          If it angers him?

Cat now turned away from the wall and looked intently at Janet.

                    JANET
          It will not anger him.   He will
          understand. I will not run and I can do
          him more good… free.

He left the room and walked to the truck using its radio to call in and have Janet's message relayed on. By midday, Mo got a response that he shared with all.
                    MO
          (Reading the Lords response)
          If they each vow loyalty to me, your Lord
          King and promise not to try to run, the
          chains can be removed.

Cat is the first to speak up…
                    CAT
          I will never promise to not run from that
          bastard.

Janet walked over and slapped her to the ground.

                    JANET
          Then stay in those chains for the rest of
          your life. I will make such a vow to him.

Janet turned to Mo, her eyes bright blue and full of fire.

                    JANET
          Tell him I will always be loyal to him and
          I promise not to run.

The other women are stunned that Janet got permission, but like Cat, they would not take the same vow. Mo walked out to the truck with Janet in tow and removed a large hammer and a chisel. He then walks to the rear of the truck and as Janet followed the others came out, all but Cat. Mo went down on one knee and took Janet's foot and placed it on his other knee. He then had Janet place her ankle next to the heavy iron bumper.
                    MO
          Don't move, this may hurt.

                    JANET
          More than it has?

MO
(Looking up)
Yes.

The first of several good whacks sent agonizing vibrations of pain up her right leg and the first rivet was broken. Janet's first shackle was off and Mo rubbed her red and sore ankle as though his large callused hands could lovingly brush it all away. It did.

She rested her hand on Mo's back as he proceeded to remove the other from her left leg. He stood up and smiled, as Janet untied the rope around her waist that had been holding up the chain from hitting the ground. It hit the ground with a thud. Mo then handed the tools to Ter and then he and Janet walked away.

JANET
(Grabbing Mo's arm)
Oh my God, I am so light. Hang onto me or
I will float away. I had no idea how used
to them I had become.

END SCENE

EXT.   MACHU PICCU - DAY

Janet and Mo took long walks together each day, but tried to stay close, because there were babies due any day. They would stop and take time to enjoy the view as Mo told of all his adventures here in this sacred land, and how the reincarnated protégé King led his teachings whenever he was around. This was a magical place filled with thousands of years of history. As they neared the end of the trail and the small structures they now called home came into view, one of the women came running up to them…

> **WOMAN**
> Hurry! She is having a baby and I know nothing about this. A woman is here to help, but she is having trouble. She has been in labor for hours now!

Janet started to run…

> **JANET**
> How many hours?

> **WOMAN**
> Close to four now!

As the last of the day's light streamed in, Janet ran to the mother and could see the baby was twisted inside. There was a lot of blood and she was burning up with fever. Janet started barking out orders as she twisted the baby with her elbow on the mother abdomen, then reached up and helped twist the newborn more, then pulled him out.

In moments it was over and the cries of new life filled the room. There was much joy as they cleaned him and Janet turned back to the mother. Pat, the mother, extended her arms to hold her new child as they all helped clean things up, Janet washed up as Mo came over to whisper to her…

> **MO**
> Is he a healthy baby?

> **JANET**
> Yes. Is it a water baby? No.

> **MO**
> How can you be sure, so soon?

> **JANET**
> I wiped sweat from his brow.

Sadness fell over Mo as though the baby was delivered dead. Janet gently grabbed his arm…

> **JANET**
> You don't know, he may be the one to (more)

produce ten water babies, for the genes
that are in him.

She stopped and stared Mo in the eyes.

> **JANET**
> (Sharply)
> Is this your baby?

> **MO**
> (Looking down with a snap in his eyes that
> quickly softened)
> No, it is not mine. Remember I told you…
> you were my first.

> **JANET**
> (Gently took his hand, looking down)
> I have been lied to so much in my life… it
> is hard for me to trust. I am sorry.

They embraced for a moment then Janet got back to work. Pat was still
losing a lot of blood and needed a transfusion. Janet was doing her
best to care for Pat, but there were no medical supplies.

> **JANET**
> Nothing… not even a good first aid kit!
> Who is responsible for this? She needs a
> hospital, there is little I can do but try
> to stop the bleeding.

Janet stayed up most of the night with her, but finally fell asleep.
It was the next morning when someone yelled out…

> **WOMAN**
> Janet, something is wrong! Come quickly!

But it was too late, Pat was gone and they had a newborn that needed
help. Once more Janet started to take over.

> **JANET**
> We need to get this infant to a hospital,
> stat!

No one moved, until Mo walked over and put his hand on Janet's
shoulder…

> **MO**
> There are no hospitals here.

> **JANET**
> (Snapped)
> Yeah, great! It looks like we're our (more)

own hospital now!

Janet stood up and looked hard at Mo who was lighting some of the only candles in the room.
> **JANET**
> We're going to need supplies quickly or this baby will not live 24 hours.

> **MO**
> You have to tell me what you need and I will get whatever I can.

The lady from the village below, Paba, gently took the baby from Janet.
> **JANET**
> The mother still has some milk, it will do for a short time.

The lady then told Mo where in town to get some of the supplies Janet called for and he raced out into the morning. Each took turns sitting with the child as the mother was prepared for burial. Mo returned with many people from the village below. Ter had returned the truck, so Mo had to walk like all people there. He told them what had happened and they all jumped in to help.

They brought food and milk and a crew to help clean things up. The small cluster of buildings near Machu Picchu was abandoned for hundreds of years, but now had many improvements underway. Within days it became a model village. Roofs were repaired, a new outhouse was built and there was one new grave.

It was too small to even be a village, but Janet thought it needed a name; so because it was below the kingdom, it should be like a queen, so she named it Curaca.
> **JANET**
> (Smiling as she stroked Princess)
> It's a fitting name for a place to have your babies.

Princess was about to deliver by the warm fire. She is a good mom and in less than an hour Princess safely brought into the world six reproductions of Prince and Princess.

END SCENE

INT.   CURACA — 30 DAYS LATER

There was now Janet, Cat, Dye and Linda. Dye came with Pat, who was now buried on a hillside and Dye had not gotten pregnant yet. She was having trouble with the whole thing and missed her lover, Pat. She told Janet she was a lesbian and wanted nothing to do with this man that came once a month and stayed for a week or two.

Janet tried to help but words could not lessen her pure grief over the loss of her lover, Pat, and to think of his next visit, this man that rapes her, is too much to bear.

When he arrived Dye ran out the back door and up into the woods. Janet told him to give her more time and explained the trouble she was having. It crushed him, for he too was under orders and Janet could see he was like Mo, sensitive. Janet thought…

                              JANET   (V.O.)
          *These men are not American men… that's for
          sure.*

Then there were loud voices from some distance, trying to get help. The men ran over to see what was going on. They were getting ropes and heading off to where Dye had last been seen running. Word spread quickly; Dye had jumped to her death. Janet ran over to the cliffs edge and stood next to Mo.

                              JANET
          This is my fault! I should have watched
          her closer. I have failed as a nurse. I
          should have spotted the signs, but I
          thought she just needed more time to grieve
          over the loss of Pat. I thought she would
          come around.

Mo grabbed Janet by the arms…

                               MO
          Stop it! No one knows when another wants
          to end their life. We all should have
          watched her closer. Her love for Pat was
          greater than we all thought.

Looking deeply into Janet's eyes Mo held her close to his face…

                               MO
          If I lost you, I too would find it hard not
          to join her, jumping over the side to my
          death to be with you.

Mo gently released Janet as the sounds of the others trying to retrieve Dye from her place of departure while they both looked on. Janet touched Mo's arm, then squeezed it firmly…

JANET

What will Our Lord think? Will he be angry
over the loss of two gifts in such a short
time? We should prepare.

Several hours later the men returned with Dye's badly beaten body.
The women laid her out as the men dug her grave next to Pat's. The
gentleman that was her lover, was devastated at the loss and stayed
at her gravesite for hours, then simply disappeared with his grief.
His grief was not over the loss of Dye's life, but the loss of his
opportunity to breed and pass on his genetic heritage, thus
preserving it for the future… as his Lord ordered. Janet watched
Linda closely and she knew it.

LINDA

I know you're watching me and you are right
to, because I may be next. You like it
here. This kind of a life is ok for you,
maybe even better than the one you had
before, but not for me. I will do anything
to get out of here! Anything, do you
understand?

Janet turned to Mo and softly said…

JANET

You had better put this one in chains like
Cat and get them both a collar chain and
fix them to a post.
     (Then Jan turned to Linda)
Stop fighting everyone and everything and
I will try to stop him from raping you,
deal?

Linda sat back and said nothing as she looked into the fire. Janet
then turned to Ter…

JANET

You did your job and she is pregnant, so
leave her alone.

He stepped out of the room and returned to his home after fathering
two gifts.

END SCENE

INT.   CURACA – DAYS LATER

                              MO
              It seems that word has spread that you can
              mend people. The sick from all over are
              showing up at the door every day!

The others soon started helping with what they could as payment. Cat
was the last to offer help, until she saw a sick child that stole
her heart. The small gathering of people became the only hospital
within a hundred miles.

In her off time, Janet would try to spend as much of it as she could
with Mo, as he would show her the remains of their history. He
promised one day to take her to the Panaca and show her what only
the very few had seen, the mummy of the king God, Pachacuti.

Janet's new companions were Prince and Princess. She taught them
how to play. It was hard at first, but they started to become dogs
after some time. But Princess could not leave her nest and could
not travel. All the puppies were fine, except for the one that could
not walk and play like the other puppies. When the others would get
away and be under foot, this one would only roll after his brothers
and sisters. Mo offered to drown the bad one and Janet would not
hear of it.

                          JANET
              Life is life and we all have a right to it!
              Whatever the outcome, it's ours to live.
              I will not give up on any life.
                  (She looked down on the pup in her lap)
              His name is Roller, and he will walk and
              play, like the others one day.

                          PABA
              No one feels like you do. It is a sick pup
              and it is cruel to let it live in a body
              that was not working right.

Janet would rub the pups back every day, stretching out his legs,
until one morning, six puppies were playing outside in the grass.
It was then that Mo took Janet's hand and said…

                              MO
              I will never doubt you again. You really
              are a God, sent from the heavens.
              Apocatequil is in your hands. I saw it in
              your fingers as it brought the healing
              power back into that pup's body. How else
              could you do so much good and help all
              creatures as you can?

Janet looked up at Mo and said…

                    JANET
          I only rubbed his muscles and loosened up
          his spine so he could move the way the body
          is meant to. What is Apocatequil?

                     MO
          Apocatequil is the God of Lighting. It is
          in your fingers. I could see the sparks;
          I could see the power passing through you
          from this God. You have that power in your
          hands.

Janet thought that it was time, so she took Mo's hand and placed it
on her belly and smiled up at him.

                    JANET
          I hope it's a water baby.

Mo's eyes filled up with tears from the news as he rubbed her small
swollen belly. She was just starting to show.

An old man was there with pneumonia and was recovering. Soon he
returned home telling everyone, of the miracles he had seen. Word
spread of the gifts from the Gods that were in the hills and that
miracles were performed for the sick. He told how he saw her rub
on a dog and made it well and walk when it had never walked.

                   OLD MAN
          Apocatequil is a real God and is back with
          us up in the Huala, the sacred place called
          Curaca.

END SCENE

EXT.   THE PYRAMID IN FLORIDA – NIGHT

The news of Janet's healing hands made its way to the Lord; who at this time was overseeing the reassembling of the black towers and the pyramid down by the sea. Lord had received a grant from the federal government of the United States to build the first in Florida. But that was only a con to get the money.

He then, in another con, sold stock in a corporation he had created that held the patents to get more money. The design worked and it took off like wild fire. He had manufacturers building them all over the world and the money was pouring in faster than he could count it.

The gold and other stolen goods from their Inca past were delivered to Machu Picchu in a single container, left at the foot of the site in the empty parking lot. With the income from the power plants the Lord could buy back stolen treasures and gold and silver bars to be forged back into their lost stolen art.

Word spread of the return of the God King and how he was here to rid the land of the evil that had taken over his people. The ruling government saw this as a threat. They did not want to give up their power.

By then the Lord King had a lot of power and could buy anyone or anything and he was not about to let anyone take it away. The president of the country increased the tax on the electric power and the Lord retaliated and gave the power away to his people without charge. The people loved him and started to look to him for leadership… not the corrupt government.

For the first time in years, he returned to Machu Picchu alone. For days, he walked the sacred site, until Tup-Con and Lee-Yaa tracked him down. Tup-Con was the first to enter his rooms, alone she kneeled in his presence.

TUP-CON
My Lord, they are going to kill you.

Lee-Yaa came in and joined her on her knees.

LEE-YA
We have come to warn you that there is money
on your head.

It was dark now and they could barely see him sitting at his desk in the shadows. He was not saying a word. The cold night air was causing the girls to shiver as they knelt near the doorway. He signaled them to come to him and they shared their warmth. He looked out the doorway to the moonlight thinking of the events yet to unfold. Like a good leader, his mind was always on the future of his people, not himself. The next morning he laid out his plans with his most loyal people around him.

LORD

> From my years in the United States of America, I learned much, and the one thing I gained was the understanding of how to control the government. We are going to have a coup, just like their President Kennedy.

Within days, plans were set in motion and a time was picked to kill their government's leader. It was to be the president's vacation, as the whole family was on their yacht, explosives were detonated and the whole family was lost to a terrible accident on the high seas. The torture was to end and political prisoners were to be released.

At that very moment, the vice president's daughter was nabbed at her school and taken away in a white van. Hours later, she was delivered to the front steps of her home. She was naked, covered in black dye and in chains. She also carried a message that read:

Stand in my way and you're next.

The following day the tax on electric power was repealed. The weight of all the responsibility was wearing on the Lord and he tried to pass off some of the load to others. The Lord called for his most trusted people and his dogs. A man in a truck showed up to pick up his companions Cusi and Urpi.

For his efforts to retrieve Prince and Princess they gave him a guarded welcome and he left with new holes, (from sharp teeth) gifts from the canines. Tup-Con and Lee-Yaa were given the task and had help from the man that had failed. The next day, they appeared and were able to take both reluctant animals. The puppies were now big enough to be weaned.

Janet had homes for all the pups and started to give them away. Prince and Princess were not warmly received and in the dead of night, they returned to Janet and Mo. The girls were infuriated and followed the tracks of the dogs back through the hills to the new hospital.

The girls told the Lord of what had happened and he seemed not to really care. They wanted revenge and he wanted nothing to do with it, remembering that he was not there to care for them all the time.

LORD

> They are free to go where they wish. I know they are happy here in our land.

END SCENE

INT.   JANET'S HOME – 3 DAYS LATER

Janet picked up Roller and spoke to MO…

> **JANET**
> Would you take Roller to Our Lord with this
> note?

My Lord,

This is a gift from Cusi and Urpi.   You own nothing until you set it free and it returns to you.   His name is Roller.

Janet

Mo left and delivered the pup and Janet's message to Our Lord. The pup was welcomed and the next night Prince traveled the path back and stayed with our Lord. He would move from Janet's side to our Lord's side, as though he had two families that he must now care for. He would check on both each day.

INT.   MACHU PICCHU – DAY

The Lord took Janet's words to heart for her gift. Roller was there every day to remind him of his real goals and the first of his decrees were ordered.

> **LORD**
> My first decree is that every mayor in
> every village/town is to clean up the drug
> dealers in their area or I will. I also
> want books of our **true** history and what the
> Spanish slave masters did to us and our
> Gods, distributed throughout our land.

In one night, all the Christian churches were raided and all the gold and silver was taken as well as the priests. Their churches were all burned to the ground.

CUT TO:

INT.   CURACA – BEFORE DAWN

Janet is shaken awake to find Lee-Yaa standing next to her bed.

> **LEE-YA**
> Our Lord has ordered you to come to Machu
> Picchu. You are to appear before him
> today. Mo is to come with you.

Mo and Janet dress and hurry to the top of Machu Picchu. Many people were present when they arrived. There was fear was in their eyes and heart as they were brought before their Lord. They both feared his retribution for the loss of two gifts, Pat and Dye.

JANET (V.O.)
Would death be better than his Lords anger?

Tup-Con and Lee-Yaa greeted them and both were taken to a room she had not seen before, at the top of Machu Picchu. There, they were bathed and cleaned removing the last of Janet's blue.

Today was clearly a special event, but no one said what was to happen and no one asked. She was dressed in the finest gold cloth she had ever seen as was Mo. Both were told how to greet the Lord, where to stand when they entered the throne room.

They were walked in and both Janet and Mo knelt down before the Lord on their knees and faced down in respect for who he was. Tup-Can and Lee-Yaa were at his side as Prince and his pup Roller, walked up to greet them both. He did not scold them or stop them for they were truly free.

The room was quiet. Only the wind blowing through the halls of this sacred land made any sound. All waited as the Lord gathered his thoughts.

LORD

Janet, I have received word, many times,
that you have done much to help my people…
our people. Stand up and look at me… you
too Mo.

Janet complied by slowly standing with Mo's help and he joined her.

LORD

I want you to help me on a bigger scale by
being my eyes and ears wherever you walk,
correcting injustice or unfairness. You
will keep me on the side of right while
caring for the sick and the weak. You both
are to be my emissaries of good will. Will
you accept this responsibility to all the
people?

Janet knelt back down in respect, surprised by the responsibility and power.

JANET

If that is what you wish me to do, then that
is what I will do and gladly.

MO

I will gladly take on that responsibility
my Lord and thank you for the trust you have
shown in me.

LORD

Good, then it is decreed, this day you two are to be Pachacutec, one who changes the world. I hope for the better… that is my wish.

They both remained standing and bowing to the Lord King.

LORD

Then stand at my side with the others.

There were others also dressed in gold standing on both sides of our Lord. It was his plan to return justice to the land and reclaim that which once was. The Lord then turned to one of the newly empowered and asked…

LORD

Is it all ready?

The man nodded his head yes and pointed to the court yard. With two claps of his hands he gestured them all out the main door and they complied as the others, now in gold followed.

The courtyard was filling with people from all over the country, as the Lord moved center stage to another throne. Silence fell over the crowd; all were on their knees in respect. The Lord waved them up on their feet and all eyes were on him. Christian priests were then lead in from the back. There were 87 of them brought before the Lord naked and in chains, then forced to the ground. All their gold and silver religious artifacts were brought forward and dumped on the ground at the feet of our Lord. Each priest held to the earth with a foot of their new masters on their necks.

As he sat on his throne, his most trusted standing at his side, he held out his hand to Tup-Con and she placed in it, the gold chain Janet had given Mo to give to him. He then looked to Janet as Lee-Yaa nudged her and she approached the Lord. He handed her the gold and she looked over at the pile then walked slowly and placed it in the pile. It slid down making the only sound she could hear and she returned to her place by his side. Janet then knew how powerful such a small thing could be. Silence fell over the courtyard as the Lord rose to his feet, pointing to the sky with one arm and to the priests in chains with the other.

LORD

Behold, the tables have turned! I bring before our Gods… in the heavens above me… the emissaries of the ones that murdered and enslaved my people and stole our wealth. They are the ones that tried to destroy the memories of our Gods and my people's love for them. You (more)

> murdered us if we did not take in your god,
> your Spanish god, and now it's your turn.

The first priest was led to the altar and tied in place. Tup-Con and Lee-Yaa stood at each side of the Lord, dressed in gold much like his, only each had red marks on their faces. Janet had seen these marks before as he sat back down on his golden throne. Prince joined them as Roller his son, stopped his play in the background, sat and watched. From behind them came two men also dressed in gold each carrying a large sword, their faces covered by a gold mask. They slowly walked up to the altar and stood at the side of the priest, not saying a word. Then the Lord clapped his hands twice, Prince sat down at his side as the first swordsmen began to speak…

MAN WITH SWORD
> I am a direct descendent of the son of Tici
> Viracocha.

It was a voice Janet had grown to know, it was Mo.

MO
> The ones your Spanish all but killed off
> as you spread your plagues of diseases and
> your Christian ethics of your gods over our
> land. You gave each a choice. Now, the
> same offer you made to our people we make
> to you. Accept our Gods and give up your
> gods or we will chop off one arm at a time.
> That offer is being made to you now, give
> up your God or Gods and accept ours and you
> can live.

The priest began to say the Lord's Prayer and with two claps from the hands of our Lord, his arms were cut off. He was then tossed to the ground to squirm and bleed out as the next was brought to the altar and made the same offer. He too received the same punishment refusing to denounce their Christian gods.

Only the very few and handpicked were chosen to witness the revenge of Pachacuti. Their Gods and souls of the loyal ones that paid with their lives at the hands of the Spanish Christians were to be present. The priest now all lay dead at the Lord's feet, as all watched with quiet joy. The Lord rose to his feet and pointed to the edge where the blood was draining.

LORD
> Toss them over and take them to the city
> of the dead.

He then turned and walked back into his palace. Janet followed silently in his footsteps as he stopped at a doorway and without turning around he asked…

LORD

What is it Janet?

JANET

Your health… I worry over your health.
You put me in charge of the wellbeing of
all and I want to check on yours.

He gave a long sigh and let her check him.

JANET

Your bites have healed nicely, but you need
rest. Try to get more sleep at night.

His old soul was in a young man, but this body was aging quickly. Janet was done and stepped out silently. Each person present, including Janet, helped move the newly dead, over the side and down to trucks waiting below. Bloody foot prints covered the stones as each took pride in the wearing of Christian blood. Several hours later they arrived at a great crevasse that opened in the earth during the last earthquake. It was there that the bodies were unceremoniously dumped. The afternoon sun dried the blood and soon the cleansing rains came and washed what remained of the Christians to the valley below. **Revenge was that of Inti.**

By then, the word had spread across the land that the Christian leaders were gone and our Gods were angry over the people's abandonment. The old ways were coming back as the term Spanish, to describe their culture was abandoned.

LORD

You are not Spanish, you are Inca! Bring
back into your life, your Gods… not theirs.

INT.   BELOW MACHU PICCHU   DAY

Word spread of the appeasement of the Gods and the miracles of Apocatequil, the god of lighting, in Janet's hands that took place at Machu Picchu and word traveled across the land to other countries.

Cat had a healthy baby boy, but sadly it was not a water baby. Janet was not far behind and Mo was at her side all the time now.

Janet was now having trouble walking and had to spend most of her time in bed, relying on others to help. But each day she would try to see each patient in their care and all the new ones, with Princess at her side.

Then it happened, her water broke and someone was waiting no more. Right there on the floor she delivered a healthy baby boy to the loving hands of Mo. Tears of joy filled his face as he looked at Janet.

MO
(Holding up their baby)
You did it! You have given us a water baby boy. He is the first! My son is the first!

News traveled quickly to the Lord King and when they could travel he requested their presence at Machu Picchu. A celebration was planned.

This time the streets of Machu Picchu were lined with flowers and smiles from all the people there to take part in the event. Janet could see the river had been dammed to save the dwindling water and to produce electricity for the palace. Janet, Mo and the new one were taken to rooms just off the main square.

Once there, they were given baths and dressed in new hand spun gold. Janet led the presentation to the feet of the Lord King and on her knees, laid the baby at his feet. Tup-Con and Lee-Yaa were there also at his side dressed in gold. Behind his mask Janet could see a smile in his eyes. Prince was there, as well as a young Roller, at his side.

The Lord King shifted on his throne as he looked at the newborn and held out his hand to hold him. Janet quickly rose to her feet with the help of Mo and she handed him the child. As he looked down upon him he said…

LORD
Do you know what this means? Your clean new blood and healthy DNA, a gift from the Sun God Inti, will be passed down in his descendants, protecting him. A return of the ancient near extinct water people, almost killed off completely by the Christians will return to our land. A totally unique type of people found nowhere else in the world but here and we have another new one, a very special one. I will call him Yapanqui, son of water.

The Lord King named their child, a great honor to be bestowed on them. He gently handed the child back to Janet, who noticed small cuts and scratches on his hands. Roller is sitting next to Prince with a toy by his side and Janet knew then the Lord King was learning the value of play, which is a sign of trust. She returned to her place on her knees next to Mo. The Lord King looked around at all the smiles.

LORD
The Gods brought us this new life and once more we all will enjoy the love they have for us. We will return to the ways (more)

of the past. They explained it to me in
a vision long ago. That vision they gave
me as a child is here now as you all see
it. This is just as they meant it to be.

He clapped his hands and the crowd cheered for joy. There was
dancing, drinking and celebrating. The next day Janet explained she
had to return to the hospital. As she and Mo walked past the newly
dammed river she pointed and turned to Mo…

JANET

We could use some of that power for the
hospital.

Someone overheard them and the next day wires were being strung.
Before the end of three days, lights were in every room of the Hospital
for better care and in all the surrounding homes. At the end of the
first day, power was in Janet's home and she took a shower in the
tepid water, dreaming of a water heater. The sounds of her child
crying after such a long day were painful in her ears. Memories of
her mother's voice came bellowing back into her mind. Janet began
to tremble uncontrollably as memories of every beating, came racing
back over her body. She took control, wiped her eyes and finished
drying, then put on her robe. Slowly, Janet opened the door to find
Mo was sitting on the edge of their bed holding their child giving
him comfort that she could not.

Janet stood in the doorway, and watched the two of them in gentle
loving splendor. The new one was falling asleep in Mo's loving arms.
He got up to put him in bed without noticing that Janet was watching
intently. Mo turned to see Janet watching from the doorway and he
smiled…

MO

We have light. Things are getting better
just as I promised you.

Janet's not saying a word took the smile from Mo's face…

MO

What is wrong?

Janet still staring into Mo's eyes, slowly closed the door to their
one-room, stone walled, windowless home, now filled with the
brilliant white light from one light bulb, hanging in the center of
the room. She slowly walked over to Mo, never taking her eyes off
his and stood in front of him as her toes dug into the earth floor
of their home, trying to think of the words. She reached up and
gently put her hands on both sides of Mo's neck and spoke softly…

JANET

I can't do this.

Mo's heart started racing in his chest, his eyes widened as he put his hands on her waist.

>   MO
>   Do what? You are a magnificent woman that
>   can do anything. What is it that you can't
>   do… is it me?

Emotions raced through his mind. Janet took her hands back from Mo's neck, and as he tried to hold on to her waist she gently pushed him away. Now standing in the center of the room just under the light she removed her robe and set it on the table.

>   JANET
>   What do you see?

Mo's eyes began to fill with tears as the unknown raced through him.

>   MO
>   I see a beautiful woman that I love with
>   all my heart and the mother of my child…
>   a son.
>   JANET
>   (Staring into Mo's eyes)
>   Look closer… what do you see? You have
>   never said a word and we have never spoken
>   on this, what do you see?

Tears now streaming down Mo's face, the words would not come out. Janet continues in a harsh monotone voice he does not know…

>   JANET
>   Touch them. Put your hand on each one and
>   tell me, what you see… what do you feel?

Mo complies with her demands and gently touches the first scar on her back running his fingers down its jagged memories.

>   JANET
>   (Continued in her harsh tone)
>   What do you see, what do you feel?

>   MO
>   (Struggling to get the words out)
>   Pain… much pain.

>   JANET
>   That is where my mother used a claw hammer
>   to open up my back. I don't know what I
>   did to deserve it, I only remember the
>   pain. After two surgeries most of the
>   scar tissue was removed. It is much (more)

better now than when they first found me.

Mo's hands were trembling as he stood there not knowing what to do next.

                              JANET
                             (Snapped)
                        Touch the next one!

As gently as Mo could, he complied. She told him of her memories of that one as well and they moved on to the next. With each of the passing memories of her torturous childhood her voice returned to one that Mo knew. On his knees now looking up at Janet, he had saved the scars on her ankles for next to last… Raising his head up to look at Janet with a smile, he touched the stretch marks on her belly

                              MO
                    Some of these are because of us and this
                    is one from me and your son. You carry
                    much of life's bad and good on your surface
                    for all to see.

Janet smiled back at Mo touching his shoulder as he tried to understand, saying…

                              MO
                    Whatever you think you can't do we can get
                    past it together.

He then embraced her thighs pulling her very close to him.

                              MO
                    Tell me what it is that I can do to help.

Mo remained holding on for dear life, as the last of Janet's anger slipped back into the dark cracks of her mind…

                              JANET
                    I can't do it. I can't do what you can do.
                    I was not given love as a child and I cannot
                    pass that on, if it is not in me to give.
                    I only have anger when I should have
                    patience and love. This is what I was
                    given as a child. I do not want to pass
                    on the hate and anger that was given to me,
                    to my child. You must stand in front of
                    my mother's anger that still resides
                    within me. You must protect our son from
                    her… for she will strike and I don't think
                    I can hold her back all the time. This is
                    why I never had children, never wanted to
                    pass on the evil that was given to me.

Mo stood up and embraced Janet with relief, lifting her off the floor…

MO

> I thought it was me you could no longer
> stand to be with.

Janet was dangling in his arms.

JANET

> No… not you. I could not imagine life
> without you, now.

The little one let it be known that he too was in the room and needed attention. Mo set Janet back down on the earth floor and picked up his new son. He sat down on their bed holding the child as he held out one arm to Janet to come join them. She slowly walked over and sat down on his lap and both gave comfort to the new one. Shared joy is double the joy. A sorrow shared is half a sorrow.

END SCENE

EXT. MACHU PICCHU – MORNING

Mo and Janet were becoming well known for having received rich gifts for the hospital and the golden clothes given to them by the Lord King. They did not think they would need a safe place to keep them and who would want to steal gifts from a god?

However, word got out about the gold now being openly stored in their room without windows and the gold at Machu Picchu. The dopers moved in for what they thought would be a quick cash score. Princess caught two of them and under the Lord King's orders they were to be brought before him.

The Lord was sitting on his throne outside on a brisk morning looking down on the thieves with contempt. Their bruised, battered and bloody bodies were naked and in chains at his feet under the guards control. With their faces held down to the floor by the guard's feet, Tup-Con and Lee-Yaa read to the Lord their crimes against the Huaca (sacred place) and how they were sent to find and steal the gold and they showed their confessions to the Lord King.

He looked, then pointed to the pile of gold in the corner of the room next to him and spoke softly…

> **LORD**
> Life is easy. You can be happy or sad, you can contribute or you can take. It takes the same amount of energy, but comes from within the spirit of each of us as to which path you choose to travel.
> You have chosen to take from others, like the Christians, and your type is not welcomed on our land. We need to purge your type from our Huaca and it is my decree that your physical bodies should not go to waste. Let your departure from this land send a message to others that wish only to take. Let's feed the ants.

Our Lord had much on his plate and did not have time for such things. He was running an empire and his time was better used for planning the future of his people. Crimes against his people that followed, or did not follow the old and true gods of this land, were dealt with swiftly and harshly. However, if you still followed the gods from outside this Huaca, you received no justice from our Lord/King. He therefore, handed out the rules for behavior and the punishments for violations.

They were drug to a tree in the forest by their chains and together, hung by their wrists over a large fire ant nest. Their leg irons drug in the nest stirring up the ants. Tens of thousands of fire ants climbed the chains and slowly covered the two dangling men.

Their cries filled the valley and brought joy to all that could hear. Their agonizing death was to take eight hours and all of it posted live on the internet. This was to be a warning to all that wished to pursue this type of life, and a notice that drugs and crime will end in this, the Lord's kingdom.

LORD
For the good of all, I will not sit back
and let you live among my good people.

The next day armies of followers gathered up many of the dopers and drug dealers and took them to the city for the Lord King's justice. One at a time, they came before him sometimes with the police to speak. One man was not a drug dealer, but was proven to have been falsely accused by another. That person took his place. At this time, only the drug dealers were marched to a second altar close to the city of the dead. The same fault and opening used for the priest.

Tied to the altar, their arms were hacked off and still alive they were tossed over the side, their limbs soon would follow. Moans could be heard as more and more came. The hatchet men had to be relieved, they could only hack so long and chopping up people is hard work. There were plenty of volunteers to replace the tired. Victims were first in line, mothers that have lost sons, then fathers, all had their turns for revenge.

This ritual went on for days that turned into weeks as the prisons were emptied of the same type of unwanted criminals, and were put to death. The stench of the dead brought all manner of living creatures to feast and finally the line of the executed came to an end.

Before long most crime was a part of history, like the Christians. The old god's were brought out of their safe guarded places for all to see and know of their returning power. Farming, caring for each other, the land and education were the top priority. All feared the Lord King, and they loved him as well. The land became a good place to live and all crime virtually disappeared for fear of the same fate as the dopers.

Janet had only to point and say what she wanted and it was done. First, the buildings and caves were too small to care for all the sick coming in. Grateful people helped build new buildings and it kept growing.

A year had passed and the hospital had two volunteer doctors. More and more of the sick and desperate came to them. One day, a shopkeeper from a town near them came with a sick child. The shopkeeper's name was Huance (god of nature) and his boy's name was Con (god of rain). On the father's arm was a tattoo that drew Janet's attention. The child was only sick from food poisoning and was

better the next day. As they were leaving Janet remarked how she
liked the art work on his arm and the color.

HUANCE

> My father did the work. You can stop in
> anytime and he will make any design you
> want. He is very good, the best in our
> land. You come see him and be my guest.
> I owe you much.

Janet had not been out of the small circle of people around her for
a long time. She wanted to see more of her new country and adopted
people. The idea struck a chord and she agreed to come for a visit.
Things at the hospital seemed to be running themselves and Janet knew
that she was pregnant once more. She said to herself…

JANET

> If I am ever to see this land and these
> people I need to do it now before I can't
> travel.

So one morning she announced she was going to go to town for a visit.
Before leaving she made sure to tell Princess to stay and that she
would be back or they would get very upset. Princess would not hear
of her leaving without her. She had to be tied up and Janet could
hear her cries as she headed down the road on foot. Five minutes
later, Princess was by her side, with her rope dragging on the ground.

JANET

> Ok, if you want to come that badly, but you
> must be good.

The road was rough with large potholes made by years of use. Dark
green canopies created by trees covered the road in places, looking
like caves cut into mountains, the land had a quietness about it that
was just what Janet needed. She first encountered a farmer in the
fields waving at her saying hello. Then a person walking by that
knew her by sight. She ran up taking Janet's hand, dropping to her
knees and thanking her for what she had done in the past to help her.

As the town got closer, there were more and more homes on the horizon
and the people were coming out to meet her, bringing gifts of flowers.
An old man down on his knees bowing to her yelled out…

OLD MAN

> She is a god, show her more respect!

The others soon joined him and her path was lined with flowers and
people on their knees bowing to her. The emotions of seeing people,
all people giving her such praise, such respect and honor was too
much for Janet. She was overwhelmed with tears…

JANET

Please get up. I do not wish this, please
rise.

They all remained in place. Janet walked over to the old man and
knelt down on her knees in front of him and softly spoke…

JANET

Please get up. I am not a God.

The old man lifted his head just a little…

OLD MAN

We all know the Gods sent you here. You
have brought us all such good.

JANET

But I am not a God!

OLD MAN

Then God's power runs through you. We all
have seen that power and know of it. His
lightning is in your touch.

He remained on his knees and would not move. Janet rose to her feet
and continued walking on the dirt road. She was overwhelmed at the
poverty and yet things were clean. As the road continued, some of
the buildings grew to two stories and there she found the store she
was looking for.

She was welcomed in by Huance the proprietor, and offered food and
drink. Janet told him of her effect on the people and that it was
not her wish to appear to be more than a person.

HUANCE

Let me walk with you. I will show them you
are just like us.

He grabbed Con's (his child) hand and out they went back into the
streets. He saw the people had thrown flowers in the street for Janet
and the ones remaining, returned to their knees and bowed.

HUANCE

I can't stop them.

Then Janet got an idea as she was looking in a store window.

JANET

Well, I will just go shopping and show them
that I am just human.

She stepped past the respectful people and into a shop.

> **JANET**
> I like those sandals you're wearing; do you
> have them in blue?

A surprised woman rose to her feet still trying to show respect.

> **WOMAN**
> No ma'am, but my father makes them and you
> need only show him what you want.

From a dark back room smelling of leather, an old man with a small hammer in his hand yells out…

> **OLD MAN #2**
> Yes, pick out whatever you want and I can
> make it.

Janet picked up Huance's arm and showed him his tattoo…

> **JANET**
> See this blue? This is what I want.

Her piercing blue eyes stared back at the old man.

> **OLD MAN #2**
> I can have them for you in a few days.

> **JANET**
> Good. Thank you.

She turned with a smile and headed out the door.

> **OLD MAN #2**
> But first, I will need your size.

She stopped dead in her tracks in the doorway…

> **JANET**
> Oh yeah, that would help.
> (Turning to Huance)
> It's been a long time since I have been
> shopping… seems like a lifetime.

Janet was taken to the back room for a fitting and sat down near the cobbler's bench. The smell of leather filled the dark room as Janet looked at all the pelts hanging on the walls and rolls stacked in every corner. She lifted her left foot across her right knee and started to brush the dust and mud from her foot.

JANET

Let me wash first. I did not realize how
I must look from my walk.

The daughter quickly handed her father a bucket with water and a rag.
As she washed her foot she was aware of the calluses on the soles
of her feet.

JANET

(Smiling up at the cobbler)
Look at that, I have been without shoes for
so long I have pads like my dog!

When she finished, he knelt down and had her stand on some paper and
he marked out an outline of each foot. As Janet watched him, his
callused hands gently rubbed her feet as he marked the paper. Years
of working the leather were in his hands and they took on the look
of the leather he had handled. Then she noticed her clean white
skin next to his brown leather skin. She thought…

JANET V.O.

*I must look like something from another
planet to these people.*

Janet placed her hand on his hard shoulders, smiled and thanked him
once more.

JANET

Now how much do I owe you?

The old man remained on his knees bowing to her.

OLD MAN #2

Nothing, for it is I that owes you.

Janet then recognized him as the one with pneumonia from her clinic.
She patted him on the shoulder, starting to understand these simpler
people and accepting her place among them, then thanked him once more.
She turned to look down the hallway lined with shoes in the light
from the street and saw twenty sets of eyes staring back that quickly
vanished.

JANET

Now who sells fabric?

The daughter also on her knees looking to the floor, pointed down
a side street and Huance knew just where to take her. There Janet
showed the lady what color she wanted and drew out a simple one piece,
slip-over, dress she designed. Janet then picked out a blue robe
that was close to what she wanted.

JANET

Now I want to pay for this.

WOMAN #2
(Smiling back)

You have already.

This is not what Janet wanted and she reached in her pocket and laid
some money down on the counter. The woman looked down in horror.

WOMAN #2

You are a god, and this is my gift to you.
You have helped so many of our people in
this town, it would be so wrong of me to
take money.

JANET

Then use this money for good.   Help
another that needs help. Buy food to feed
the poor.

The woman smiled up at Janet and reluctantly accepted the coins.

JANET
(Turning to Huance)

Let's go see your father now; I now know
what I want.

Returning to Huance's home where a large table was being set up in
the main room.

HUANCE'S WIFE

You, of course, are staying for dinner and
I have drawn a nice bath for you, so you
can soak for a while and remove the dust
from the road.

They were one of the richest families in town and they had indoor
plumbing of sorts. A small room in the back had a tub being filled
with hot water heated on the wood stove. This inviting tub waited
for Janet and she soaked in the warm water thinking…

JANET　　　　　　　　　　　　　　　　　　　　　　　V.O.

*They worked so hard to make me feel
welcome. How could they have known a
heated bath is just what I needed? How do
I repay them?'*

The smell of cooking food filled the air and Janet felt it was time
to get out of the tub, because the water was brown and had cooled.
As she dried off, the door opened a crack, and Princess stood up
watching intently, as Huance's wife spoke softly…

HUANCE'S WIFE

A gift has come for you.

A package was passed through the barely opened door. It was wrapped in paper and tied with a string. As Janet opened it she could see it was the blue robe from the store.

Looking down at the donated clothes she had worn here, she thought, it would be a nice change. Emerging from her bath she stood in the doorway, glowing. The father, who was old, covered in tattoos and bent over with arthritis, tried to show his respect, then took her by the hand into his shop and locked the front door.

HUANCE'S FATHER

> Good. Now you and I can talk and no one
> will disturb us.

Janet showed him what she wanted and he laid it out on her arm. By dinner time, he was half done.

HUANCE'S FATHER

> Let's eat, I will finish after we eat.

They spent the night talking and enjoying each other's company. He finished her tattoo that night. Janet was offered their bed to sleep on, but she told them she would sleep on the couch. The next morning she awoke and sat up to see a small table next to her. Folded on it were her newly sewn blue dress and her blue sandals. As she touched them she thought…

JANET   V.O.

> *They must have worked on them all night.*
> *That was a very kind thing to do.*

Looking around she saw she was alone so she slipped into her new dress and sandals. The sandals even had padding and were the blue she wanted. The same as the new blue on her arm, the same as the dye used in her ceremony a lifetime ago.

Her old things were washed and tied in the same paper used for the robe. The new dress was soft and felt good on her skin. She looked toward the restroom and thought of the hot bath she had. The smell of leather filled the air as Janet looked down, rubbing her finger tips on the stitching of her dress she thought…

JANET   V.O.

> *They're too nice to wear on that dusty*
> *road. These people have been so kind, how*
> *can this be happening to me? Me! Of all*
> *people!*

As Janet looked around she noticed movement in the street. As she opened the door she stepped out to see the whole town was there and flowers were in the street before her. They were all on their knees, bowed in respect for her… the God.

The sight was very moving and pushed Janet back in the room, where she tried to catch her breath and wipe the tears from her eyes. She gathered up her things and thinking of the road ahead removed her sandals so as not to soil them. She stood in the doorway, her toes wrapping around the sill that stepped down into the street. She took a deep breath, and then marched out the door onto a bed of flowers.

Standing in the center of the street she turned to Huance, Con and the rest of his family coming out the front door and taking their place on their knees in respect, bent over.

Janet looking down, pointing at her newly tattooed arm, revealing for all to see a slender blue lightning bolt twisting down her arm to end at her index finger tip. With the biggest of smiles she looked up to see that she was alone in her joy.

> **JANET**
> Rise to your feet. I wish to speak to your
> face.

Huance slowly stood looking at her and at the others looking down with fear in his eyes.

> **HUANCE**
> (Speaking softly)
> You are Pachacutec, (one who changes the
> world) from the family of Ayar (Sun God)
> with the Apocatequil (God of Lightning) in
> your hands, we all must show you respect,
> for you are the embodiment of these Gods.
> To not show respect is not in us.

> **JANET**
> Tell your family to rise. I wish to thank
> them.

As she moved down the road she made each person rise to their feet so she could look into their eyes and know their names. The cobblestone street returned from under the flowers and the road home before her turned back to dirt and mud. At the end of the petals, Janet turned back to see them all back in their places of respect. She returned with memories she never thought she would ever have.

That same year Cat had her first water baby, a boy and was freed from her chains. Janet had the first female water baby ever. It was a big deal and another celebration took place. This time the Lord King gave Janet a gold medallion and a paper that read,

By command of your Lord King

This person is Ayar Mamacona from the family of the Sun God and Mother/Chosen Woman. She is from our Gods in body and to receive

the highest honor and respect from all. We are to give her anything she wishes and her requests are never to be denied. This is my command and any that denied her will face death at my hand.

Pachacuti

This was a new level of power rarely given and Janet did not know what to do with such a gift. Gravel roads would be nice and better plumbing. It was done. Janet returned to Huance's father for another blue lightning bolt to circle her arm ending at her middle finger this time.

Janet was ever so careful to speak, for she did not want to regret words or speak in anger. She had much respect and power over all. There was no returning to a simple life, that life was now gone and Janet was no more, she is Ayar Mamacona.

The Lord King's power was growing ever stronger and he wanted Mo and Janet to visit the land of his forefathers in the southernmost tip of South America.

A new SUV was provided for Mo and Janet. Like any trip or vacation there were tons of things to pack. They would be gone for months and they needed to take everything with them. Even extra large fuel tanks and extra gas cans were on board.

Janet, for the first time got to see more of her new country than a gravel road, as they made their way back down to the ocean, the beaches and the salt air reminded her of the one where she had met Mo. That was a different country and different sand and a different ocean. Still, it is a remarkable land and brought its own new joys.

The country today is called Chile and they passed the Punta Arenas on route 9. For the most part, it is a harsh barren forgotten land with little to offer but cold, wind and rocks, Janet thought, but she said nothing. The road ended in San Juan, where the rest of the trip was to be by ship.

The second night out, the captain had to find a cove with protection from the winds. The captain used eight anchors to hold the ship in place and keep it from crashing on the rocks. The night was long with hurricane winds that blew at over 100 miles per hour and lasted the whole night. Few got any sleep.

Not many people lived in this harsh environment and the towns grew smaller as they headed south sometimes with dead ships of the past pointing the way. A string of islands dotted along the coastline and the captain followed them closely, pointing out sights to Mo and Janet, as he does his best to fish as well as be a tour guide at the same time.

Janet counted only nine small towns of less than 100 people before they got to their destination, Cape Horn. She insisted that he not tell them of their status, for she wanted to see these people as they truly were. Not bent over on the floor.

JANET
I want to be treated as one of them or at
least like a visitor… not a god.

There, Mo met several of his ancestors as they hunkered down for another big blow. Gale force winds blew for hours then stopped. Janet remarked…

JANET
No wonder the trees are bent over and there
is no dirt, it all gets blown away.

It was their fourth storm and the worst. Most all of the people were Yaghan, an indigenous people that have lived on this, the most southern point of land in the world. Today, it is called Cape Horn by the Christian Spanish, but these people have lived here for over 10,000 years. There are several indigenous tribes living in these parts and Janet was warned to not mix them up, for it would be offensive. Some still speak the Yamana language.

They were short in stature and wore few clothes. Sometimes sitting in close cluster for warmth, Janet thought. They were from another time, living off the land as they had for thousands of years.

JANET
The gods must be strong here.

The Yaghan people were kind and giving. They were taken back by Janet, who is fair skinned, blond and blue eyes. The locals thought her reactions to the winds were funny, saying that she will get used to it. They stayed in one of the old stone homes used for rare visitors.

Much like their home, only bigger, with no windows and one heavy wooden door braced to keep out the powerful winds. The floors were stone and there was no fireplace for heat, because there are no trees. Janet felt this stone floor was moving up in life.

Each day, when they could and the winds would slow, all the towns' people would gather in a type of main hall. Janet had counted less than thirty people total living here. There was the business of life. Most struggled and worked hard to keep things going here at lands end. The sea was in all the faces of the elders, for all made their living off the sea in this windswept land.

Janet could often feel the eyes of people on her because of her fair skin, blond hair and bright blue eyes. She was a sight among the others and most truly believed she was the daughter of their sun god. She seldom spoke, for all within the sound of her voice would stop and hang on her every word. They were words from the gods and must be given such total respect.

Janet was once more special, unique and stood out from all the others. The only time in her life she was able to blend in was working at the hospital. There, deep in her work, she was just another nurse and could be part of something. Before, she stood out… special… as a survivor. Even in her work there were the stares and whispers behind her back. But deep in her work, she was a nurse and could hide. Now she was once more special and unique and was standing out alone. Janet kept to herself most of the time, but when the doors were closed she had Mo, who understood, her son, Yup, (Yupanquc, Son of Water) and the newest little bundle of joy, her daughter, Par (Paryaqaqa, God of Water).

Janet was becoming a good mother and love was in her all the time, if she could just keep her mother locked behind that black door.

Word of the Lord King's power had even reached this tip of land and the good he had done was known. A visit from Mo and Janet meant a great deal to these people. For the Lord King knew of them and cared for them. They too were part of his kingdom and were not forgotten. The old Gods were returning and the proof was in Janet's eyes. Janet had to behave properly and not bring shame onto Pachacuti, the Lord King God.

The Yaghan spoke of the winter time, when the people would break the ice to swim in the water and kids would play in the freezing cold air with no clothes on. Then the elders spoke of a time when the Christians came and told their people to cover their bodies. When they put on the clothes they would get wet and the people got sick and there was much death.

YAGHAN TRIBESMAN
We are glad the Christians and their gods
are gone. Now we are free to be Yaghan.

They were all so open and easy to speak to that after a short time you felt like one of them.

When they had first arrived, they were given a welcome celebration in the community center. People from all around attended and Janet counted a total of 43, including the four of them.

They had stayed there at the Horn for two months and 18 storms, exploring their rich history. Time was growing close to winter and they had to leave or end up staying for the next four to six months. Plans were made for their departure; all that was needed was fuel for the boat in order to return. A tanker was overdue and without it they were stuck there.

Then the cold winds started to blow and the sea turned to ice, they were locked in. None of the radios worked this far out in these winds. The elder woman among them was also the mystic and she was calling out for help. Word spread that they could not leave.

ELDER WOMAN

No one can leave! We are the only ones left!

They tried to calm her down and pull her out of her trance, but she drifted in and out of consciousness. One of the elders got on his short wave radio again and tried to reach someone. A nearby ship responded.

SHIP'S RADIO OPERATOR

Looks like some kind of outbreak. You're better off staying where you are. We are heading for a port north of here. We will call you back with word a week from now at this same time.

As hard as they tried to reach others and get more information, there were only a few ships that responded and then none. The week went by and they could not reach the first ship. Only silence was on the cold windswept air.

Days turned to weeks, weeks to months. Winter had set in early and hard. All the people helped one another and everyday they tried to reach someone. But as the old woman said…

ELDER WOMAN

You can't raise the dead.

INT. STONE HOME – DAY

Mo and the elders made plans to get back to Machu Picchu to discover what has happened. They made plans to fit the SUV with a larger CB radio antenna when they got to the first out-post for fuel.

MO

I am sure we can make it. If there is no electricity we can use this hand pump to bring up the fuel from the tanks.

The sea started to open up and the winds died down, giving relief as the sun came out in all its brilliance. There short summer was coming and the gravel beaches opened up and filled with seals and walruses, their main source of food.

JANET
When we get back I want to send these people
vitamins and greens, fruits and
vegetables. I am surprised we have not
seen scurvy running rampant here. They
are healthy, but I fear heavy metals are
in them from living off the sea. We will
test all of them. I have to tell you I am
sick of seals and walruses!

Mo smiles and agrees. Then the subject turned back to what happened.
They headed out and at the same time each day they would radio back
to camp from ship to shore. The gale force winds made for slow moving
as they made their way north. The winds blew the fallen snow into
rolling balls of blinding and hypnotic light before their eyes. It
is still winter in these parts and these storms are what ended the
life of these great ships that sprinkle the shoreline from time to
time.

Each of the nine small towns who were also recovering from the dark
winter, the captain would stop to check on their well-being and to
see if they had news. But they also were wondering what was going
on. Each day they reported back, and their news was passed on from
short wave to short wave and back to Cape Horn.

At the foot of the Punta Arenas, near San Juan they got a broken up
report on the short wave radio of massive death across the world.
As they neared this town, there was no sign of life, but their own.
Finally, they made it up to the dock of a town of less than 300 people.
No one came to meet them, as the captain tried to raise the last broken
up voice. Mo wanted to enter the town and Janet tried to stop him,
but Mo said…

MO
If it is going to kill us let's get it over
with. If there are people we can help,
let's help them.

Janet stayed with the kids as Mo walked the town, all were dead. A
newspaper in the store told it all on the front page.

Chile News

Cure For Cancer
Is Cause of Deaths

*The race to cash in on the 'one shot fits all' cure
for cancer is traced back to India. The Sacred Monkey
Research Institute of New Delhi, India created a so called
vaccine to end all cancer. Causing a flesh eating
bacteria with an appetite for all cancers was a
breakthrough and worked well at first on all skin cancers.*

Soon it was upgraded to an oral vaccine and was widely used as the breakthrough.

Its uses spread over the globe and was declared safe for all to use if handled properly. But, as we know, bacteria can mutate and this one did. It started in India as a mystery illness and was discovered to have symptoms of a cold that turns ones lungs to mush and you drown in your own blood. It then quickly spreads throughout the body, devouring all meat.

It became airborne and within six days has spread over the globe. All planes were grounded, but it was too late. Several nuclear plants are reported manned by the dead and have exploded sending radioactive gas into the air. Avoid all these sites.

By now Janet and the kids had joined Mo, for they had to retrieve their SUV if they were going to head north. There was a sound coming from the back room as a man approached them.

                         MAN
              You're alive! I am not alone! Are there
              more?

Janet and Mo were startled as they looked at the man.

                          MO
              Yes, south of here. You are the one we
              spoke to on the short wave.

                         MAN
              Yes! It comes in the air. But why did it
              not kill me? And why are you still alive?

Janet and Mo looked at the man as he continued…

                         MAN
                  (Pointing out the window)
              Right after the truck with my store
              supplies arrived, people got sick
              including him. That's his truck there.
              If there are more alive to the south I am
              going there.

And out the door he ran to talk to the captain of their boat. They gassed up and headed north trying to reach people on the CB. After several days, they began finding small clusters of people. Janet was keeping records and counted 73, including the ones they left at the tip of the horn.

It was becoming clearer to Janet that the survivors were all South American Indian with high cheek bones and dark brown skin. She shared her news with Mo, telling him that she may be next and that the kids would be all his to care for, if this did not take them as well.

As they approached the last big town before Machu Picchu, only a handful of people were there and they were so glad to see them. That's when they were told about Pachacuti. He was dead.

In silence they drove past the abandoned buildings to the lot below his palace and parked. Others had followed them and when they arrived at the base there were more people, frightened and looking for guidance. Looking up to Machu Picchu, they were greeted by two very hungry friends Prince and Roller, near starvation.

They were doing their job, guarding the Lord's home. Janet and Mo fed them and they were joined by Princess in a joyous reunion. Silence fell over the crowd as Janet looked up the path holding onto their children. One person spoke up…

LINDA

> Let us take the kids. The dogs know you
> and trust you. We will care for them until
> you return.

EXT. MACHU PICCHU - DAY

Janet and Mo proceeded up the path finding not a soul or hearing a sound. As they looked in the palace of the Lord King Pachacuti, they saw no one. The dogs lead them to the courtyard where the body of our Lord was drying in the sun.

Tup-Con and Lee-Yaa were at his side thin as rails, guarding the King. When they spotted Janet they both dropped to their knees and bowed.

TUP-CON

> Our prayers are answered. The Gods
> returned you unharmed. Now we have
> someone to lead us from this time of death.

Janet looked at Mo with a shocked expression.

JANET

> What happened to our Lord King?

TUP-CON

> The news of his people cursed him. He
> would not get out of bed or eat. So we did
> not eat. Then he died and we did what we
> were trained to do. His body was dressed
> in his finest of gold and laid out to be
> dried in the sun.

Lee-Yaa pointed to the sky as Janet looked up, it was brilliant blue, the same blue as on her arm.

LEE-YA
No planes to fill the sky with poison that
blocked the sun.

TUP-CON
It's going to get hotter he told us. What
do you wish of us?

JANET
First rise to your feet and look at me.

They did as she ordered and their eyes reflected the lost souls within, their bodies trembling from lack of food.

JANET
I order you to eat. These animals are in
your care. They belonged to your Lord
King, you will show them more respect as
you will your own bodies. I need you alive
and healthy. Not dead!

They both dropped to their knees looking down to the stone walk.

TUP-CON
But there is no food. We are here alone.

Mo told them of food in the car and he helped them down the path so they could eat. Janet started to enter the palace, first removing her blue sandals and walked gently over the stones feeling the cool smooth workmanship under her feet. She slowly neared the throne the Lord ruled from and lovingly touched the arm rest where he once placed his hand, as though that would bring him back... or closer to her. Her sigh was the only wind as she listened intently for movement from Pachacuti... for some sort of sign.

For the first time, she entered this back room that was once the Lord King's chambers. It was dark and hard to see, but slowly Janet could see piles of books in neat stacks on the floor. She found books on mathematics, engineering and science, plus she counted seven languages. Also in the dim light, Janet could see notes on a small table with a backless stool nearby.

The room was sparse and plain. No rugs, no art on the walls, only a simple wooden bed with a thin mat. The bedding was soiled as though unwashed for years. Like the room of a monk... it was plain and simple. The God King Pachacuti lived like a poor man. Janet thought...

JANET   (V.O.)
All this time I thought he did this *(more)*

for the money, to empower himself.   But he
spent next to nothing for his own needs.
It was all for the people… his people.

Janet bent over the table and finally sat down on the stool.   There was a lamp and power still ran from the dammed river.   In the piles of papers on his desk she found his diary filled with more notes. As she sat and read for hours, she was overwhelmed as to how he was able to stay on top of so much.   Between the lines, was a troubled man filled with worry over whether he was making the right decisions for his people.

There were countless notations of dreams he had and messages from the Gods.   He referred to them as mystic messages and mentioned several living mystics and their books.   The notes read…

I understand how they received messages that they did not understand.   The cars filling the streets not moving, was one that was received over one hundred years ago.   Mine is a recurring dream of small gears resembling the workings of a clock all scattered under my bed.   What could this mean?

Janet did not have an answer for him.   She gently put the book back in its place and stretched out her tired and stiff limbs.   Her toes touched something, so she looked and saw Jule's sandals.   She pulled them out and saw they were worn paper thin in places.   She placed them back, turned and slowly looked under his bed, but there was nothing.   No parts of a clock and no gears.   Just haunting silence as she reverently intruded into his life.

The sound of a baby crying grabbed her attention and she stood up with one hand on the table for support and looked out into the main hall.   One slip of loose paper from his notes had cut her finger slightly.

It was an old dark crimson red book full of more notes from Pachacuti in his own hand.   She could feel him all around her as she vibrated with his presence.   Janet opened the book to that page of loose paper sticking out so she could remove the note to read…

Ayar Mamacona,

I have failed as a leader.   One time before, I was empowered to protect them and the ravenous greed of others, overpowered me.   This time I felt sure I would succeed and push them and their all destructive lust for money away and protect my people, but I have failed again.   There are so many dead and I cannot stop them.   I just don't know what to do.   Now it is up to you.

Pachacuti

Janet (Ayar Mamacona) gently closed the book, then slowly and silently started to walk out of the Lord King's room, but stopped at the doorway. The room was full of people, all on their knees bowing to her, faces to the floor.

Mo was comforting their newest addition, standing by the Lord Kings throne. The people were not moving or making a sound. Janet looked at Mo, as tears started streaming down her face and he gave her a stern look indicating to wipe her tears away. Then he looked at the throne, pointed with his head and smiled, then pointed to the people the same way.

Janet's hands were trembling as she slowly approached, then touched the arm of the throne for the first time… as one that must guide and lead. She looked at it hard and realized what killed the Lord King, she thought…

JANET/AYAR
How can I do this?

Mo reached over and took her hand and pulled her in front of her people and her throne. She then realized she might be the most educated person of the ones remaining and best qualified to lead.

She lifted herself into the throne and realized just how hard and big the seat was. Placing her hands and arms on the chair rests, she looked down at her bright blue tattoo and wondered if the old man was still alive, for she is now carrying a third child.

As she sat there looking at the people she raised her left foot to rest it on her right knee. With her left hand she touched the scar on her arm from when her mother poured boiling water on her as a child. Then down to gently touch the tattoo as memories raced in her mind. Her right hand now rubbing the scars left from her shackles, she thought…

JANET/AYAR   (V.O.)
Where do I go from here?

THE END

www.ingramcontent.com/pod-product-compliance
Lightning Source LLC
LaVergne TN
LVHW062356180726
843498LV00009B/1328